The Two But Rule

The Two But Rule

Turn Negative Thinking Into Positive Solutions

John Wolpert

WILEY

Published by John Wiley & Sons, Inc., Hoboken, New Jersey.
Published simultaneously in Canada and the United Kingdom.

ISBNs: 9781394221080 (Hardback), 9781394220885 (ePDF), 9781394220878 (ePub)

For general information on our other products and services or for technical support, please contact our Customer Care Department within the United States at (800) 762-2974, outside the United States at (317) 572-3993 or fax (317) 572-4002.

If you believe you've found a mistake in this book, please bring it to our attention by emailing our reader support team at wileysupport@wiley.com with the subject line "Possible Book Errata Submission."

Wiley also publishes its books in a variety of electronic formats. Some content that appears in print may not be available in electronic formats. For more information about Wiley products, visit our web site at www.wiley.com.

Library of Congress Control Number: 2023916900

Cover design: Wiley
Author Photo: © John Wolpert

SKY10061264_112823

To Amy, Catherine, and William.
You are behind my every intention.

And to the constant readers of 2buts.com.

Contents

Introduction   *xi*

Part 1   **Momentum Thinking Essentials**   1

Chapter 1   Embracing Your But   3
                Our Broken Buts   5
                Two But Basics   7
                Stating the 1But   9
                Stating the Because   11
                Stating the 2But   12
                Elon Musk's Fuzzy But   13

Chapter 2   No Buts Allowed   17
                The Tragic Buts of Facebook and
                    Lehman Brothers   18
                The No-Buts Policy Makes Dumb
                    Ideas Stupid: Ask Coke   19
                Spanx, Adobe, and the 1But Winner   20
                We Need Bolder Buts   22
                Building Braver Buts   24
                The Science of Buts   26
                Waiting for the Quantum But   27

	Saving But-Head	28
	Rescuing 1But-Guy	30
Chapter 3	This Book Saved My But	31
Chapter 4	Getting Your But in Shape	35
	The Pain in Your But	36
	What's Behind Your But	38
	Best Buy's Big Buts	39
	Uber's Bigger Buts	41
Chapter 5	Advanced Butology	45
	Gnarly Buts	45
	Chain of Buts	48
	Rediscovering Your But	53
	Proteins Got a Brand New But	54
	Hidden Buts	56
Chapter 6	Bad Buts	59
	Lewis and Clark's Historic Buts	60
	Cheating Buts	63
	Volkswagen's Gassy But	64
	Don't Be a Lazy But	66
	Don't Argue with Your But	66
Part 2	**The Two But Rule in Practice**	69
Chapter 7	The Social Life of Buts	71
	Drunken Buts	72
	The Gaps in Your But	73
	Exposing Your But	75

Chapter 8	Playing with Your But	79
	Timing Your But	82
	Butting In	84
	The Odious But	85
	The Empathetic But	86
	The But of an Ass	87
Chapter 9	Old Buts and New Buts	89
	Airbnb and Paul Graham's Old But	
	Breakthrough	90
	Runaway Buts	92
	The End of Buts	95
Chapter 10	Putting Your But to Work	97
	Leaning Into Your But	99
	Five Buts	101
	The Two But Retrospective	103
Chapter 11	Managing Your But	105
	2But Tools	106
	Two But Notation	107
	Artificial Buts	107
	Two-But Buddy	109
	Protecting Your Buts	111
	Teaching AI to Embrace Its But	112
Part 3	**Life's Big Buts**	113
Chapter 12	You and Your But	115
	Everyday Buts	116
	Fixing the Fan	117
	Surviving Parenting Purgatory	118
	Changing Careers	120

Chapter 13   Business Buts   129
                 Running a Small Business Is a Pain in
                     the But   129
                 Calendly and the Many Buts of
                     Starting a Business   133
                 Where to Sit Your Buts   138

Chapter 14   Product and Technology Buts   145
                 The 2B Product Review   146
                 Who Owns Your But Online?   146
                 Product Feature Creep   151
                 Regulating AI   155

Chapter 15   Buts in Conflict   163
                 Solon, Father of Buts   163
                 Big Government's Budget Buts   168

Chapter 16   Saving the World...with Your But   175
                 Windy Buts   176
                 Plastic Buts   178

Chapter 17   The Rear End   193
                 The Buts We Leave Behind   194
                 Embrace Yourself   194
                 All Your Wonderful Buts   195

Acknowledgments   197

About the Author   199

Index   201

Introduction

We're in trouble. The world feels like it's coming apart. And every solution, every innovation, seems to deliver a truckload of new problems. We're in fight-or-flight mode all the time, driven by fear. Fear of the unknown, fear of seemingly insurmountable problems, and fear of each other. Some of us respond to this by clinging to blind optimism, some wallow in obstinate negativity, and some offer half-baked ideas and censor those who question them.

This book offers an alternative, a way out of endless, circular arguments. It offers a path to solving impossible problems and capturing opportunities beyond our wildest dreams. To do that, we must rediscover an asset that most of us have been sitting on our whole lives.

This is your guide to discovering the positive power of negative thinking. We're going to dive headfirst into the benefits of contrarian perspectives and challenge the way we react to them. We'll traverse the spectrum from blind optimism to obstinate negativity and find the sensible middle, where innovation and practicality don't have to be at odds. We won't be wallowing in negativity. Instead, we'll harness it and turn it into an engine that drives us toward better solutions and better understanding of the problems themselves.

This is the practice of Momentum Thinking, or, as I like to call it, *The Two But Rule*. Momentum Thinking is a way to tackle complex problems and opportunities without slowing down or ignoring issues. It's not a miracle cure or an overnight transformation but a useful habit of balanced, nuanced, and innovative thinking.

Part 1 of this book covers the essentials of Momentum Thinking, guided by vivid examples, engaging stories, and some admittedly adolescent humor. We'll review catastrophes caused by failures to apply the Two But Rule and successes of those who, consciously or unconsciously, applied it well.

Part 2 shows how to put the Two But Rule into practice on teams and how to turn Momentum Thinking into *Momentum Doing*. Then we'll explore important techniques and tools (including the use of artificial intelligence) to help remove some of the frictions that can hinder the practice.

Part 3 puts it all to the test on life's toughest problems, from the personal to the professional to some of the biggest challenges facing humanity.

Why is all this crucial for you? Because the world isn't getting less complex or uncertain. You're going to need a way to find clarity amid chaos, see opportunities where others see dead ends, and make connections in a world that seems more divided than ever. This isn't just about problem-solving. It's about harnessing the potential within you and the people around you to create lasting, positive change.

So, if you're ready to grow your capacity to see problems clearly and to solve them creatively, it's time to unleash the power of the Two But Rule—not just for you but for a world that needs a new burst of momentum.

Be sure to join in our community of innovators and problem solvers at 2buts.com. And for more support and tools for applying Momentum Thinking to your life and work, visit TheTwoButRule.com.

Momentum Thinking Essentials

1

Embracing Your But

Something's on your mind. You've got things to do and problems to solve. We're not talking about the simple stuff like deciding to take a break from social media. We're talking about the complex, high-stakes stuff like starting a company when you're broke, studying for exams while working two jobs, or re-creating Grandma's famous holiday stuffing without the recipe. Whatever it is, you're stuck, and you're searching for a way to figure it out.

In that search, you're going to come up with a lot of dumb ideas. If you don't, you're not doing it right. That idea you had in the shower this morning? Yeah, not good. Don't feel bad. It's just not good *yet*.

You're not alone: YouTube started as a video dating site. PayPal started as a way to beam money between Palm Pilots. (Remember Palm Pilots?) Sparkling Champagne began as a fermentation accident that caused bottles to explode. And my first attempt at re-creating Grandma's stuffing involved dousing it in vodka.

(After I worked my way through the liquor cabinet, bourbon was the answer.) These are just a few of the countless cases of getting smart by starting dumb.

Overcoming seemingly impossible problems and creating truly innovative things depends a lot on how much momentum you can muster when turning bad ideas into good ones.

But standing between you and the promised land of solved problems and glorious achievements are a bunch of meddlesome other people—and one particularly meddlesome person inside your own head—who are going to slow you down, trip you up, and send you crashing into a dead end. And they'll use one powerful, much maligned word to do it: *but*.

"But that won't work." "But it's too expensive." "But we have better things to do." But, but, but.

You probably don't like the buts. But, you should. In fact, if you want to have the best chance of success in whatever you do, you need to embrace a lot of buts. And that's the funny thing about them: even though a single one will stop you in your tracks, buts can really generate momentum when they come in pairs.

Momentum Thinking That's what the Two But Rule is about. It's about turning the world's biggest idea killer—and arguably the world's biggest relationship killer—into a powerful tool for getting unstuck, building velocity, staying nimble, and even repairing relationships. It's a tool that's always with you, though you rarely look at it, and you have to be mindful about how you display it in public. Yep…it's your but.

You might believe that you know your but, but you don't. There's a lot more there than you think. Throughout this book, we'll explore many useful kinds of buts, how to get them into shape, when to reveal them, and why it's essential that all buts come in pairs.

This is the basis of the Two But Rule: following "But that won't work" with "BUT it would if…" will lead reliably to more positive outcomes for you, your ideas, and the people in your life. Like a Shakespearean comedy, applying the Two But Rule starts out negative but turns positive in the end.

If you're a leader, a scientist, a general *pain in the but*, or just a regular person facing tough choices and hard problems, the Two But Rule is for you. If you're none of these, it should also be a mildly amusing digest of "*but* jokes" for adolescents of all ages.

There's a lot more to executing the Two But Rule than its simplicity suggests. Keep reading. You might discover some surprising things about buts and how to handle them.

Our Broken Buts

NASA Flight Director Gene Kranz never said, "Failure is not an option." That was a line delivered by Ed Harris in the 1995 movie *Apollo 13*. In fact, during the tense days in April 1970—when an oxygen tank exploded in the service module taking astronauts Jim Lovell, Jack Swigert, and Fred Haise to the moon—failure wasn't just an option. It was a likelihood.

What Kranz did say was this: "Let's solve the problem, people. But let's not make it any worse by guessing."

Solve the problem. Don't make it worse. It's a different way of looking at things than we've seen lately in technology, government, and society. Gig economy startups bulldoze whole service sectors while losing vast amounts of money simply papering over the same old problems with new buzzwords. Rash and reactionary government policies sacrifice human decency and common sense to satisfy the demands of an angry political base. Social networks and decentralized financial platforms claim to be about community and inclusion but instead deliver devastating blows to social norms and further concentrate wealth in the hands of elites.

These are the products of a no-buts-allowed culture, where the powerful, perhaps frustrated with the general pace of change and seemingly intractable problems, plow ahead with half-baked plans. They believe it's too hard and time-consuming to understand context, learn how the status quo came to be, or consider the consequences of their actions. All this underscores a deep misunderstanding we've developed about innovation and momentum.

"Move fast and break things," Facebook's motto until 2014, set the tone for this approach to "disruptive innovation" that persists to this day. It suggests that deploying new ideas fast without taking constraints into account is better than sitting on your but pondering what to do. And at a high level, that sounds reasonable. But the things we're breaking these days are becoming hard to fix. We need a better way.

It's worth noting that the Apollo 13 team had no time to spare in saving the crew, and yet they didn't just move fast and break things. They moved even faster to identify problems, offer ideas, consider new problems presented by those ideas, and manage a complex array of constraints until they had plans that worked. They were engineers and scientists, with plenty of skeptics who didn't hesitate to point out the flaws in a plan. But they also had the mental fortitude and camaraderie as a team to say, over and over, "But that won't work, BUT it would if…." This is the Two But Rule.

For example, when the damaged Apollo 13 command module ran out of life support, the three crew members moved into the two-person lunar module, but the CO_2 scrubbers were inadequate for the increased load. Left unfixed, the crew would have died of carbon dioxide poisoning. The command module's scrubbers could handle the job, but they needed to be fitted to the lunar module's round ports…and they were square. So the ground crew figured out how to fashion a makeshift connector from duct tape, plastic bags, and parts from a spacesuit.

They applied the same approach when they discovered a problem with navigation, a serious problem with the power supply, and issues with restarting the dead command module when it was time to re-enter Earth's atmosphere.

In more than one case, a contrarian viewpoint averted further disaster. An initial plan to use the main engine for a direct return to Earth was scrapped in case it had been damaged in the explosion. Later, when they ejected the service module and observed the actual damage, it was clear they had made the right choice.

In another case, flight controller John Aaron directed the team's attention from other problems to the spacecraft's dwindling power supply, convincing them to cut power in time to have enough battery reserves for re-entry. And later, he threw out the standard playbook and ordered an unorthodox power-up sequence. If he hadn't, the ship would have run out of its remaining battery power before reaching home.

Every time they found something in a procedure that wouldn't work, they found a way to make it work or to approach the problem in a new way. Fortunately for the crew, what they didn't do was ignore the skeptics—or let skepticism bring them to a halt. For every "But that won't work" (1But), they found a "BUT it would work if…" (2But) and then repeated the cycle, always matching a 1But with a 2But, a 3But with a 4But, and so on. Failure, it turns out, is only an option when you stop on an odd-numbered but.

Two But Basics

We've been moving fast and breaking things for a long time. And now, we're faced with problems so big, complex, and immediate—from climate change and social unrest to the rise of our AI overlords—that our only option is this: Solve problems. Don't make things worse. And somehow move faster than ever. This is what Momentum Thinking is all about. So let's get into some details.

Momentum Thinking starts when someone presents a problem to solve or offers an opportunity to capture. In either case, someone is forming an intention.

For Apollo 13, the intention was clear: *bring the crew home safely*. The priority was unambiguous: *scrap the moon landing and bring the crew home safely*. And the immediate nature of the emergency focused the minds of everyone involved: *bring them home safely before they run out of life support*.

These three factors made it more likely that the team could overcome the fact that they had no idea, at first, how to pull it off. It's not always that straightforward. Intentions, especially early intentions, are as delicate as they are packed with potential energy. They can be tricky, and we'll talk a lot more about them later.

The Two But Rule is all about how we keep momentum flowing without ignoring problems with those early intentions. It starts simply enough. Whether in a meeting, a formal brainstorm, or just sitting with yourself thinking through a problem, you allow the phrase "But that won't work" (a 1But) to be said in a thoughtful manner after an intention has presented itself. But, only on the condition that it is immediately followed by the phrase "BUT it would work if…" (a 2But).

There are variations of this:

"But *I don't like that, BUT I would if….*"

"But *we can't afford that, BUT we could if….*"

"But *you're a big dumb poopy-head, BUT you wouldn't be if….*"

Stating the 1But

Here's an uncomfortable exercise, if you're up to the challenge. Keep track of how many times you say the word *but* over the course of one whole day. If you're an overachiever, note what you were reacting to, how you were feeling at the time, what argument you were presenting, and whether in retrospect your assertion was objectively true, based purely on belief, or completely full of sh*t. Oh, and mark whether, after presenting your but (your 1But), you followed up with any second buts (2Buts).

Given that *but* is one of the top 100 most frequently used words in the English language, you'd be doing well if your count were less than 50. And you might start to notice some things about what motivated you to use the word and where the conversation went after you did.

Ideally, we present our buts as a way to show contrast, consider exceptions, and identify constraints. Assuming your motivation is to seek truth and achieve a productive outcome, it's useful to consider whether your but is refuting an assertion or trying to refine it. Regardless, it's critical to be clear-eyed about whether your but is expressing an observable truth, an unprovable belief, a sense of skepticism that can be tested, or just a contrarian habit. (If the latter, keep reading. You still have a chance to be the hero of the story.)

Here are a few more variations of 1Buts:

But I just don't know.

But I don't believe it.

But that violates my beliefs.

But I want something else.

But I don't like/trust/know you.

But that won't work technically.

But that won't work practically.

Some 1Buts are pretty easy to handle. For example, "But I'm not sure I understand what you meant" can be followed with "BUT let's try again." Likewise, if there's a clear problem with an idea that can be solved in a way that doesn't involve unacceptable trade-offs, then you can say, "But that material won't work, BUT we could use this other material instead."

On the other hand, assertions based on beliefs can be the hardest buts of all, and we'll dig into them after we've mastered the art of the Two But Rule. There really is a way to achieve Momentum Thinking and find solutions that work better for everyone, even when conflicting beliefs seem intractable.

Another difficult 1But makes assertions that can be proven, but the time and effort required to find the truth exceed the willingness of anyone to spend it. Sometimes a little consideration is enough to find sufficient evidence or logic for both sides to agree on the point. But if the original idea (or your 1But) isn't worth testing to establish a reasonable sense of truth, you have to consider whether it's worth the effort of "butting in."

Finally, there are 1Buts that you may just want to avoid. Chief among these is the dreaded "But what about?" A close cousin is the "But that won't completely solve the problem." If you identify a problem to solve and the argument to *not* tackle the problem is based on a claim that it will still be a problem in other contexts, then you have hit a 1But wall and may simply need to find someone else to problem-solve with.

That said, when you've mastered Momentum Thinking, you can sometimes find powerful clues into real problems and solutions hiding in someone's "What about…." They might really be saying, "But I don't want to" or "But I don't feel like it."

They might not want to admit, even to themselves, why they don't like your idea, and that itself is interesting and potentially useful. They might really be saying, "But if you solve that problem, my profits will go down…but I can't say those words even to myself, so I'm going to find some other reason to oppose the idea that sounds better to my ego." All of these are clues to find better solutions.

Stating the Because

Figuring out whether you're starting with an easy but, a hard but, or a but full of hot air starts with one word: *because*. If you're presenting your 1But, be sure to add it. And if someone is baring their 1But to you, be sure to ask for it. It's simple:

"But I don't like that idea, because…."

"But I don't believe you, because…."

"But you're a big dumb poopy-head, because…."

You have to admit that, even in the last case, the *because* can really help with presenting the argument thoughtfully.

The *because* is also helpful for finding an interesting 2But. For example, you might say, "But I don't want to spend money and time on a book that boils down to a two-line aphorism and some potty humor, *because* I'm busy working at a job that doesn't pay me enough." And then you might say, "BUT maybe I could read this book, become a Two But guru, build a following of loyal but-heads, and launch a successful consulting career."

Did this thought just change your life? Yeah, perhaps not. But finding a second but, even a silly one, can provide a real jolt of mental momentum. And that's what we're looking for.

Stating the 2But

There are perhaps as many variations of 2Buts as there are combinations of intentions and 1Buts:

There's *The Lay-up*: "But I don't understand how this will work, BUT let's figure it out."

The Punt: "But we just don't want to do something new right now, BUT we could do it later."

The Jab: "But you're wrong, BUT you wouldn't be if…."

The Mentor: "But we tried that in the '90s, and it didn't work, BUT here's what went wrong so you can avoid this mistake when you try it again."

The Scientist: "But your conclusions are flawed, because your data are inaccurate, BUT we can still explore your hypothesis if we construct a better experiment."

The Engineer: "But that idea won't work the way you think, because you're not considering the weight load these cables can bear, BUT we could use a higher tensile strength cable instead."

The Accountant: "But this is going to cost too much, BUT we could eliminate your salary to cover it."

Endless variations.

At this point, you might be saying, "I get the idea, but there are plenty of times when I simply can't think of a good second but." You're in luck! There's a 2But even to this but: BUT you don't have to provide a particularly good second but.

In Chapters 5 and 6, we'll get into some of the finer points of producing a well-formed 2But, including how to look for hidden buts, avoiding bad buts, and managing long chains of buts.

For now, let's talk about my favorite: the silly but and its variants, the crazy but and the fuzzy but.

For example, a team of newly hired MBAs and engineers at IBM were brainstorming ways to approach a new project. One of the MBAs proposed a plan. An engineer curtly said, "But that won't work." When asked to add a second but, the engineer said with a grumble, "Well, it would work if gravity worked differently." A classic silly—maybe in this case, *snarky*—2But.

Not five seconds later, another engineer jumped out of their seat and said, "Wait a minute!" They then proceeded to lay out an idea that didn't alter gravity but did lead to a patent filing and a project that would later garner the attention of the company's CEO.

Sometimes the crazier the 2But is, the better. It doesn't have to solve the problem. It just has to maintain momentum. Introducing the notion of gravity to the conversation, something completely outside the context of the initial idea, gave the second engineer an unexpected insight.

Elon Musk's Fuzzy But

Crazy buts, silly buts...and now let's look closely at the all-important fuzzy but. Elon Musk's company SpaceX started as an idea to land a miniature greenhouse on Mars with the ultimate goal of growing plants there. That idea had problems. In 2001, the cost of building and launching rockets was too high, making the Mars mission unattainable for a private company. Musk went looking for breakthroughs in rocket technology.

He observed that the spot prices of a rocket's raw materials were about 2–3 percent of the total manufacturing cost at the time. That gave him the seed of an idea: design manufacturing to optimize turning raw materials into a rocket. That came with an obvious 1But: But all known methods for this process, refined over decades by some of the best engineers in the world, were still too expensive.

A technique to keep things flowing on a hard problem is to blur the lines of the initial idea when formulating the 2But, making the idea "fuzzy" and breaking it down into *first principles*. First principles is a way of thinking recently popularized by Musk but originally formulated by Aristotle. It says that the nature of a thing comes from the nature of its building blocks and how they interact.

So, using the first principles approach, Musk observed that materials are just collections of atoms. That led to an important 2But: SpaceX could cut costs dramatically if they had a magic wand for turning atoms into rockets. Crazy but? Check. Fuzzy but? Check.

It turns out that Musk did indeed have a magic wand. Three of them. The first wand was access to enough private capital to vertically integrate materials supply and production. The second wand was a new modular manufacturing approach based on the principles of Musk's prior experience in object-oriented software. The third wand was the emerging field of additive manufacturing (aka 3D printing), literally a magic wand for rearranging atoms and turning them into rocket engines.

On September 28, 2008, SpaceX launched the first privately developed liquid-fueled spacecraft into orbit, proving that a good set of crazy, fuzzy buts can launch you on a journey to outer space.

Elon Musk, and people like him, have a relentless and seemingly inexhaustible capacity for gnawing on a problem like a dog with a bone. But they also have a knack for maintaining momentum. That's the difference between dwelling on a problem and iterating through it. They bring the second but, no matter how crazy or fuzzy it is.

Applying the Two But Rule can feel like going over a psychological roller coaster. There's a moment of fear that no 2But will present itself. And then the thrill, as the mind latches onto something and gets pulled along, often on an unexpected journey. Yours might not be to Mars, but you're going somewhere.

Like all journeys, the trip can be fraught with dangers. For starters, in today's world, all buts are under attack.

2

No Buts Allowed

Have you ever found yourself in the shoes of Cassandra, the priestess of Apollo gifted with foresight but cursed so that all her prophecies fell on deaf ears? Or have you ever found yourself in a company full of would-be Cassandras, always predicting disaster? Neither situation is much fun.

It's true that cultures dominated by negativity tend to be stagnant cesspools of inaction. And habitually saying "But that won't work" will get you nowhere (and earn you a reputation as an obstructionist to be ignored), but there's another momentum killer that's even more insidious. And it's on the rise.

We live in a culture of correctness, toxic positivity, and general avoidance that leaves us utterly bereft of our buts, incapable of pointing out problems or even fully realizing there are any problems to solve. In such an environment, nobody wants to hear about your but, even if you come with two buts in hand. Call it the no-buts policy.

Admittedly, the proximate cause of a no-buts policy is usually a long-standing culture of negative 1Butism that long ago eroded the organization's ability to innovate. Unfortunately, if 1Butism is a momentum killer, a no-buts policy is worse.

The Tragic Buts of Facebook and Lehman Brothers

Sandy Parakilas was a Facebook platform operations manager responsible for protecting the personal information of the social network's users. His special focus was third-party developers that provided a variety of services—from games like *Farmville* to popular surveys like *This Is Your Digital Life*. To do this, these services accessed data from Facebook's internal systems.

For example, *This Is Your Digital Life*, created by Cambridge University researcher Aleksandr Kogan, collected data about both Facebook users and their networks of friends to generate personality insights.

Parakilas grew worried about these apps in 2011, later telling *The Guardian*, "My concerns were that all of the data that left Facebook servers to developers could not be monitored by Facebook, so we had no idea what developers were doing with the data."

He raised these concerns to management, but he says they were not heeded. He left the company in 2012.

Soon after that, Aleksandr Kogan shared the data he had collected about Facebook users with political consulting firm Cambridge Analytica. The scandal that resulted was legendary. *The Guardian* and *The New York Times* reported in 2018 that profiles of millions of people had been created by Cambridge Analytica from Facebook's data and used in a variety of political campaigns.

The fallout resulted in Facebook CEO Mark Zuckerberg being called before Congress, where they vigorously paddled his *but*. The Federal Trade Commission launched a probe into Facebook that led to a $5 billion fine. And eventually several executives found themselves out on their buts, including the CEO of Cambridge Analytica.

In the end, the whole affair led to reported changes in how Facebook and other platforms handle user data, but not before the scandal caused a general erosion in the public's trust in social media, which persists today.

In another notable case, Joe Gregory, president of financial juggernaut Lehman Brothers, famously asked, "Why bother worrying about dizzying levels of debt and exposure to potential defaults—when all good things come to those who are optimistic enough to expect them?" Lehman collapsed in 2008 and triggered the Great Recession.

Like a Shakespearean tragedy, the no-buts policy starts in a state of positivity and ends in carnage after the main characters ignore all the signs of impending doom.

The No-Buts Policy Makes Dumb Ideas Stupid: Ask Coke

Clearly the no-buts policy has a terrible effect on identifying and solving problems. And it's not just about making it unsafe to speak truth to power or raise red flags. It's often about allowing obviously dumb ideas to persist and percolate without challenge, where they eventually take root in the DNA of the organization without having been transformed into good ideas along the way.

It's especially easy for a dumb idea to stay dumb when it comes wrapped in statistics from flawed studies. A good example of this was Coca-Cola's decision to reformulate its flagship Coke product in the mid-1980s. The decision was prompted by taste tests that showed people preferring sweeter drinks. This allowed proponents to push aside resistance to the reformulation project.

But the taste tests failed to account for how preferences might change when people drank the sweeter drink regularly over time.

New Coke replaced the original formula in April 1985. The response was so bad that it led to a public relations crisis as consumers demanded the original formula be restored. Three months later, the company reversed itself by introducing Coca-Cola Classic. New Coke is widely considered one of the biggest product blunders in history.

There were plenty of opportunities to avoid the mess. Folks who weren't convinced of the wisdom of New Coke appear to have missed several opportunities to apply the Two But Rule. Otherwise, they might have been able to redirect proponents into better decisions that could have resulted in a wildly successful product instead of a costly double-rebranding exercise.

For example, if taste tests indeed indicated a preference for a sweeter drink, they might have introduced a test product in specific markets to learn how it performed over time rather than replacing the formulation of the flagship brand.

Spanx, Adobe, and the 1But Winner

The thing that leads to so many of these unnecessary failures may be a general misconception about how we achieve success. Try searching Google for "dumb ideas that led to great ideas" and most often you'll find stories of inventors and entrepreneurs who had a brilliant idea that everyone thought was dumb but that—after heroic perseverance—made them rich and changed the world.

For example, everyone passed on supporting the development of form-fitting, footless pantyhose until a mill owner decided to help with what most saw as a "crazy" idea. If we take this story at face value, persistence alone made Spanx a household name. A world today without Spanx would be unimaginable for the ranks of on-camera personalities that rely on them.

There are a million origin stories like this. Everything from bicycles to automobiles to even cheeseburgers were considered ridiculous at first. The story of the true believer who ignored the skeptics and persisted is so ingrained in most of us that it's easy to subconsciously gaslight ourselves when our inner skeptic reacts to something new. None of us wants to be the one remembered for saying that there would only be demand for "maybe five computers in the world."

Still, the mythology of dogged visionaries achieving success by clinging stubbornly to their initial ideas is as narrow and simplistic as an action movie. And it belies the fact that most of the time, when innovators ignore skeptics, their perfectly good *dumb ideas* become *willfully ignorant ideas*. Or in the vernacular—they become *stupid ideas*.

Many of these stalwart innovation myths, if you look more closely, hide details about how the original idea changed significantly on the way to success. For example, in the early 1980s, two employees from Xerox's Palo Alto Research Center, Charles Geschke and John Warnock, left to start a company called Adobe. They initially thought the business would sell turnkey computer hardware and printers. As the story goes, they pitched the idea to Apple Computer's Steve Jobs, who passed on it. But he suggested they focus on making libraries of typeface fonts and licensing them to computer manufacturers like Apple. After a year of pushing their original idea, Warnock and Geschke relented and took Jobs's advice. Adobe font technology went into the revolutionary Apple LaserWriter, and the computer graphics industry that followed made Adobe one of the biggest names in high tech.

The myth of the stubborn innovator is bio-pic magic, but if we want to solve problems in ways that have the best chance of working in a complicated and rapidly changing world, then we need to understand that the real heroic act is having the courage to refine ideas through the crucible of scrutiny and opposition.

We Need Bolder Buts

Courage. Bravery. These words might have been considered by Harvard Professor Amy C. Edmonson and team when they selected the title for their 2019 book *Fearless Organizations*. It's a good book and worth a read. It suggests that organizations seeking to promote better problem-solving, innovation, and general employee well-being must foster a culture of what they call *psychological safety*. They focus, in particular, on the fears that low-status employees have when considering whether to point out problems to superiors (or problems *with* superiors). They suggest that people often self-censor when they're afraid of losing face or being reprimanded.

While the authors take pains to say that people shouldn't be shielded from the realities of the workplace, it's easy to conclude from the book that the goal is to construct *fear-less* environments rather than to hire and foster brave employees who face their fears and voice their perspectives judiciously and cogently.

We don't want terrorized organizations run by desk-pounding bullies. On the other hand, imagine what it would be like to work in a dystopian society full of people who never think about how others might react to their comments. We need to love our dumb ideas, but innovation never thrived in a cacophony of unexamined nonsense.

Many of us can remember a time when we were the new hire or the lowest-ranking person in a team. No doubt, that situation usually involves some discomfort. You don't want to speak up because you don't want to be a big mouth. You don't want to look bad in front of the boss—or worse, develop a bad reputation with the group and get "voted off the island."

Psychological safety is important. However, the implementation of this perspective can be perilous. If making low-status team members feel safe means that leaders have to worry about how any criticism is received by any employee, dumb ideas can go unchecked. Learning is lost. Rather than the junior team member checking themself for fear that the boss might snap at them—which is definitely not OK—now we have the leader checking themself when the junior member proposes an idea or objects to a plan. The easy out is to praise the input, do nothing about it, and move on. This is the frozen ninth ring of the *toxic positivity inferno.* Everyone, juniors and seniors alike, trade becoming masters of problem-solving for mastery of the infernal art of covering their buts.

A little fear, mixed with the bravery to stand up when one has a big enough but to warrant the risk of exposing it, sets a natural balance. And this doesn't have to come from fear of reprimand. On the contrary, employees at Microsoft and IBM were known to work especially hard on honing their proposals and counterproposals for leaders like Satya Nadella and Arvind Krishna, not because they were scared of reprimands but because they didn't want to let them down. That fear didn't hamper new ideas. It made them better.

Edmonson and team briefly nod to the undeniable assertion that everyone, employees and leaders alike, must bring courage to work, but then they immediately return to the pattern of describing employees feeling that they couldn't speak up, that they felt powerless. They point to disasters caused by superiors not heeding warnings, but they fail to explore what happens when experienced people throw out their own judgment and execute the decisions of a less experienced person simply to empower them. Given recent shifts in corporate culture as a new generation enters leadership, this inversion is happening more often and deserves closer scrutiny.

There's no question that we need to foster a culture of listening, and we'll get into this in detail later. For now, consider that concerns raised by employees, colleagues, and even superiors are often overruled or ignored as a reaction to being presented with only a single but. People don't like getting a package of problems that doesn't come wrapped in solutions. Even a solution that clearly has its own problems is likely to get a better hearing than a warning that presents no path forward.

The Two But Rule makes always presenting solutions an easier habit to build, and organizations that foster this habit are places where it's easier to speak up and to listen.

Building Braver Buts

If you're working with a team that needs an infusion of bravery to get things going, here's a useful approach. Researchers from Lancaster University and the University of Illinois at Urbana-Champaign published a paper in 2006 called "Why Bad Ideas Are a Good Idea." They observed participants attempting to solve the following problem:

> *"You have 9 balls. One of these balls weighs fractionally more than the others, though you cannot tell just by holding them. You are allowed only TWO weightings using a balance scale. How can you find the heavier ball?"*

Typically a participant started by weighing four balls on each side of the scale, which is not the best approach. (The ideal starting point, it turns out, is three on each side.) But some started with clearly unbalanced configurations, like weighing one ball against eight. Surprisingly, these participants solved the puzzle 20 percent more often than those who started with a more sensible choice.

The researchers suggest that starting with a clearly "bad" idea somehow *perturbs* the participant's exploration of the problem and avoids traps that appear rational. It's a good example of Momentum Thinking. Starting with a dumb idea isn't just OK. It might provide advantages, as long as it prompts iterative critical thinking.

If you want to try this for yourself, the researchers suggest the following methodology when brainstorming:

Step 1: Ask participants to suggest a deliberately "bad" idea, like constructing a "glass hammer" or an "inflatable dartboard."

Step 2: Ask:
    a. What's bad about the idea?
    b. Why is this a bad thing?
    c. Is there anything that shares this feature that is not bad?
    d. If so, what's the difference?
    e. Is there a different context in which this would be good?

Step 3: Turn the bad idea into a good one without "fixing" the thing that makes it bad. For example, an inflatable dartboard with blunt darts, both covered in Velcro material, turned out to be a product idea during one Bad Ideas session at the Dublin Institute of Technology. The important thing is to get people taking risks and implicitly setting a context where doing so is not only allowed but seen as fun.

There is an art to this, and you need to be working with people who know how to have fun. When the researchers tried to apply the Bad Ideas approach with teenagers, the students tended toward literal interpretations. For example, they couldn't get past the fact that a "chocolate greenhouse" would melt. They couldn't produce a 2But. It suggests that applying the Two But Rule is a learned skill that requires some amount of maturity.

You need teams that can consider two or more opposing ideas at the same time and either resolve them or at least tolerate their simultaneous existence. This is what you see in outstanding creative teams. It's also essential for good science.

The Science of Buts

Science has always been about buts. It's a large part of the scientific process. Form a hypothesis and then go to work diligently trying to tear it down: "But that won't work, and also that won't work…and we don't even know how to figure out if this other thing won't work."

Rather than simply trying to prove their assumptions, scientists—at least since the early 20th century—form what's called the *null hypothesis* (written as H_0, pronounced "H-not").

For example, if they believe that a new drug candidate reduces heart disease, they'll employ the null hypothesis, which negatively states that the drug will have no effect. Then they conduct experiments, usually giving the drug to half of a randomly selected population and a placebo to the other half. If the group that didn't receive the real drug develops heart disease significantly more often than the group that did, then the null hypothesis can be rejected, and the drug trial can proceed to the next phase. Sure, this description is grossly oversimplified, but it shows how science explores the negative to find a positive result.

On the surface, the scientific approach seems pretty negative. But in a deeper sense it shows great positivity. The scientific method is expensive. It takes time. You can grow old looking for a way to run practical experiments and waiting for them to produce conclusive results. That level of diligence requires immense reserves of hope and faith. It takes patience, something in short supply in a world where both science deniers and science promoters engage in lazy, short-term thinking based on little actual evidence or careful experimentation.

Waiting for the Quantum But

Today, computers plod step-by-step through a series of ones and zeros to make calculations. Quantum computers are different. They aim to answer certain questions many millions of times faster than normal computers could. They do this by carefully preparing and measuring the properties of subatomic particles.

A manager from one of the early research labs working on quantum computers was dining out, when over the back of his booth he overheard two friends discussing quantum computing. He struck up a conversation and discovered they had just started a company to build quantum computers.

"But what are you going to do about the decoherence problem?" he asked. Decoherence refers to the nettlesome habit of subatomic particles interacting with the environment and introducing errors that render them useless.

"We're still in high school," one of them said. "We figure you'll solve that by the time we graduate from college."

That conversation happened in the year 2000. Even now, more than 20 years later, experts predict that it will take another decade or more before they know how to build quantum computers that can really do what we hope they can. They have many more rounds of "But that breaks the laws of physics, BUT it wouldn't if…" to go. The young entrepreneurs had their timing wrong, but not their faith in the tenacity of the scientists who have been working in the field for decades.

Imagine walking into a room of scientists and saying, "OK, everyone, we're going to brainstorm today. There are no bad ideas. Please refrain from killer phrases." Meaning, nobody should challenge anyone's assumptions.

They might indulge you, but they won't respect you. You've instituted a no-buts policy on people who have a long history of evidence supporting the belief that embracing their buts is the best path to developing ideas with impact.

Saving But-Head

When we fail to foster the bravery to present our buts openly, what we get instead can only be called *innovation theater* mixed with a lethal dose of toxic positivity that encourages going along to get along. Meetings run by people seemingly there to ensure that nothing is said, nothing is decided, and nothing gets done. Design thinking sessions, strewn with Post-it notes, run more to gain buy-in and sell consulting projects than to develop break-through ideas. Innovation camps and retreats featuring the pro-verbial ropes course and trust exercises. And the inevitable brainstorming session, always with the admonition "Please, no killer phrases." These momentum-free zones are where the no-buts policy reigns supreme, where everyone seen nodding their head in passive agreement gets a participation award.

Try forcing any group of employees, from scientists to accountants, to participate in any so-called innovation workshop, and then watch closely for the eye-rolling. Some are better than others at hiding it, but only the most Pollyanna-like pusher of positivity can fail to see it. These hard-core optimists believe that the hapless employees remain in the session because they like it, not because it's hard to walk out after you've removed their *buts*.

Harvard Business Review cites research showing that while "innovation" is a perennial top priority for C-level executives, the prospect is terrifying for rank-and-file employees. Fewer than 25 percent of surveyed employees aged 35 to 45 think positively about innovation programs. All this leads not to breakthroughs and sustained innovation but to a culture of cynicism that makes it even harder for any idea to grow in the parched soil of a jaded organization.

The culture-killing scourge of lazy and poorly conceived idea mining invades the organization both through grand programs and through the cumulative effect of everyday team meetings. You know the ones. A manager asks for ideas and gets back a cocktail of nada, zilch, and bupkis. And then the agony is intensified by *that one guy* who's going to ruin everyone's day by chiming in with a half-baked idea. Management then praises it while letting it die on the vine of positive, but inert, reinforcement.

Eventually, even the hand-raiser stops taking the bait, and meetings become reminiscent of Ben Stein in the movie *Ferris Bueller*, asking his drooling high school students to answer questions, repeating "Anyone? Anyone?"

The only thing worse than this scenario is when the hand-raiser is followed by someone else with the audacity to challenge the half-baked idea. On the bright side, everyone is now alert. Even the person drooling on their desk perks up. Why? Action! The chance, finally, for some forward momentum. Except for one thing. Everybody hates the but-head who just made the meeting even longer.

To be clear, *but-head's* mistake wasn't that they engaged in the conversation. It was that they offered only a single but: "But that won't work." Mic drop.

The life of 1But-guy is rough. They're habituated to challenging others' ideas, and that makes them either a barely tolerated team irritant or an outright pariah. The boss keeps them around to break up the monotony and stir the pot...until they overstep. The halls of mental health practitioners must be filled with 1But-guys. It's stressful being on the outside looking in, especially when the urge boils up to buck groupthink and point out the obvious flaws in a plan.

Ultimately, 1But-guy leaves, having been isolated and ignored even when, as we saw with Sandy Parakilas at Facebook, they might have averted disaster.

This is a gross waste of talent. 1But-guy might be annoying, but they're more valuable and far less pernicious than the no-but policy police.

This is not to say that there's no place for withholding judgment momentarily while a new idea is forming, and people should absolutely feel safe forming those ideas out loud. But in a social environment where it's unsafe to speak negatively about anything, the no-buts policy is as guilty of blocking forward momentum as the skeptic who flatly says, "But that won't work." Both are conversation stoppers. The no-buts policy, however, papers it over and makes it hard to re-engage later, resulting in a lost opportunity to evolve a good idea from the initial bad one.

Rescuing 1But-Guy

Maintaining forward momentum, that's what we're after. So how do we get it? How do we transform 1But-guy from the villain of the story into the hero?

It starts, obviously, by turning 1But-guy into 2But-guy. Sounds easy enough, right? *Just tell the hapless but-head to bring not one but, but two buts instead.* (Yeah…that's a 2But poem. You're welcome.)

It's not that simple. It certainly wasn't for me.

3

This Book Saved My But

Before we continue, there are some things you should know about me. First, I'm not going to tell you that I'm a world-class expert on managing my *but*. I don't hold the *Harold Kiester Chair of Two But Sciences* at Harvard (though I have applied for the position).

No, I'm writing this book because I could fill a castle library with volumes on how I've failed to embrace my but. How I didn't find a way past a negative roadblock. How I spent years as a but-head, followed by more years ignoring all the buts.

I've been a product executive, a startup founder, and an emerging technology scout for most of my career. I was in AI before it could tell you convincingly that it was alive. I was building mobile apps before the iPhone could handle data and phone calls at the same time. And I once tried to convince one of the founders of Google to join our Internet research lab...while he was still in grad school. (He politely turned us down and later hired a fair number of our best people.)

I worked for IBM three times and was a startup CEO a couple times. I started a multinational consortium for joint R&D a few years back. And I've held the *official* title of "Seeker of Awesomeness," not once but twice. One company put it in my employment contract, and IBM actually put it on my business cards.

Sometimes things worked out. Sometimes my thing didn't work out, but *the thing my thing was about* did. Sometimes things went in the drawer of failed experiments and are there now, waiting for someone to open that drawer and try them again.

Even with decades of experience living and working all over the world in a surprisingly wide range of fields, I still can't tell you how I succeeded beyond my wildest dreams, how I saved the world two or three times, or how I maintain such a hard and well-formed but that it could appear in a Marvel movie. And that's OK. You don't need Captain America but guy. He has no idea how to get your but in shape. He doesn't realize that showing you his workout routine isn't going to do for you what it did for him.

On the other hand, experience does count for something. True story: I took an entrepreneurship class in grad school where the professor had the audacity to announce that they were a great entrepreneurship teacher *because they had never started a business*. I'll give them points for moxie, but we weren't buying it. Now, if they had started a dozen businesses of many different types over a couple decades of trial and error, and those businesses all failed so spectacularly that they had to get a job teaching, then they might have been onto something.

Saying "I can teach you how to avoid mistakes because I have trafficked in every kind of mistake" is a claim I can get behind. It's not the blind leading the blind. It's the person who's had a broken arm showing you how to fashion a sling for your broken arm.

My whole life, the thing that got me involved in way-too-early projects, risky startups, and roads less traveled was a fascination with seemingly impossible problems. I enjoyed grappling with the nuances of the issues, the balance points, and the constraints. I have a high tolerance for sticking with a puzzle, even puzzles where it's not obvious that there will ever be a solution. I've always been more fascinated with how something doesn't work—how it doesn't work *yet*—than in how to use it as directed.

This crystallized for me when working for an innovation consulting firm in Silicon Valley. A colleague there would often say "Always but the but." That one line stayed with me, and it's led me into more trouble—and out of more jams—than I can count. It also helps me in times of transition.

In 2022, after almost a decade working on early blockchain technology, I called it quits. Blockchain is a slag heap of bad ideas buoyed up by a lot of hot air rising from a global cesspool of financial speculation and money laundering known as cryptocurrency. I had been hard at work shoveling "But that didn't work, BUT it could if…" upon "But that also didn't work, BUT it could if…" for years. Suddenly I found myself fresh out of buts.

Running out of buts on blockchain, for me, was a big transition. I was reasonably successful in the field. But I knew most of it was a grift, right down to the basics of the technology. BUT I was making really good money, which I needed to support a family. But I couldn't get it out of my head that I was the beneficiary of a speculation game that made money off the backs of so-called greater fools, duped into "investing" money they often couldn't afford to lose by people who should have known better.

That's when I came across this saying: "Misery comes from living in a manner inconsistent with your values. Despair comes when the obvious alternatives are also inconsistent with your values. Hope comes in realizing that those aren't the only options."

I might have been able to continue finding more buts to pile on the blockchain bonfire. Instead, I stopped cold, deciding I didn't want anything more to do with an industry that had beat the land speed record going from idealistic inception to irredeemable corruption and hypocrisy.

But…the problem was that I had occupied my mind so thoroughly with this topic for so long that I had no idea what else of value I could bring. BUT…but there was my old colleague in my head saying "Always but the but."

Writing this book helped me find my but again. I hope it helps you find yours.

4

Getting Your But in Shape

It's time to get our buts in shape. To do that, we have to dig further into intentions, into the moment someone decides to change the status quo and into the motives behind that decision.

If inventions are the nouns of innovation, intentions are the verbs. In fact, compared to intentions, inventions are easy. Inventions alone are inert. They can be written down, patented, and shared. But then they just sit there, idle until someone decides to do something.

For example, here's an invention:

You bore a hole lengthwise through a piece of wood, insert a shaft of graphite into the hole, and cap it with a bit of rubber on one end.

Now, here's an intention:

Someone comes along and needs a way to write something on a piece of paper, but they want to erase what they wrote later. They take your invention, whittle the end opposite the rubber to a point, and— voilà!—the pencil is born.

But then someone else comes along, carefully examines the pencil's pointy end, and shoves it into your eyeball.

Now it's a disruptive innovation.

As you can see, intentions make things happen. And they're risky to share. You can't simply patent an intention and share it, not if you want your victim to stand still while you're trying to stick the pencil in their eye.

Deciding what intentions are worth spending time on is essential for picking your buts wisely. It's also important for deciding whether, when, and how to *but* in on someone else's intentions. Sticking your but into someone's brand new intention can be uncomfortable. Certainly, it can cause anxiety. That doesn't mean you shouldn't do it. The point of this book is to argue that you should—and to suggest how it can be done in a way that builds momentum.

The Pain in Your But

Your brain is forming intentions all the time. You may not be fully aware of it yet, but stop for a second and you can feel it. You're gravitating toward capturing an opportunity or overcoming a problem. The idea is starting to take shape. You're beginning to muster the willpower to go after it. But…

It can be physically painful to have a creative idea and find yourself confronted with a giant but, a problem so huge that it seems impossible to overcome. How do you work through that pain and find your way to your next 2But?

Adam Alter recounts in his book *Anatomy of a Breakthrough* how being stuck is something everyone experiences. People of all kinds, he says, report being stuck in at least one aspect of their lives. They struggle to get out of bad relationships, move on from stagnant careers, achieve weight loss, pay off loans, save for the future, and generally find creative solutions to enduring problems. Sometimes, even when the solution is obvious, people can feel "frozen on the spot."

Just as the vision of the thing you want to make or fix or achieve comes into focus, you realize that it will come at a cost. Change always does. You go to bed dreaming of what you will do. Then you wake up in the middle of the night, sweating over the insurmountable obstacles standing between what you want to do and what you think you can do. Your buts have crawled right into bed with you.

Most people are conditioned to run from the pain, to ignore it. This is where Momentum Thinking can bring some relief. Instead of avoiding the pain, embrace it, knowing that for any "But it won't work…" that you can think of, you have a "BUT it could work if…" ready to go in your creative process.

The sharp pain you feel when confronting immediate obstacles can be exhilarating. If you don't freeze up, the clarity and seriousness of the situation can spark momentum all by itself. But sometimes the pain is just the vague sense of ambient misery as the days slip by without progress. You're stuck, and you don't even know it. You've allowed many little buts to slip into your subconscious, and now they're weighing you down like 1,000 lead balloons.

The way to handle this is so obvious that you might have to push through the next couple sentences to keep reading, because you're definitely going to say, "I already knew that."

Yeah, it's being mindful. Practicing mindfulness. Taking at least 20 minutes a day listening to your own brain do its thing. Just listening and not doing a single thing about it. Don't react. Don't judge. Don't label. Don't explain. Don't plan. Don't think about what you're thinking. Just sit and listen, maybe with a friendly, detached smile on your face to greet your thoughts and feelings. Let them know they're welcome in your brain, no matter what they feel like.

In a culture where we're encouraged to be positive, the negative buts—especially the little ones that build up—will run away from your conscious mind if they think you'll judge them or edit them. You have to go full *Jane Goodall* on those little buts. Blend in and observe.

Sometimes, the little buts aren't blocking you at all. It's just that your level of intent is too low. You may decide that the correct 2But is simply to relax and let go: "I want to become a skydiver, but I don't know the best place around here to get lessons, BUT I really don't want to go skydiving all that much."

Consciously let go of the intention, and free yourself from the low-level pain of self-recrimination over not becoming the next Tom Cruise. In the process, free your mind to tackle intentions that really matter to you.

Paying attention to your own intentions and facing the gaps between what you want to do and what you can do is important. Why should others listen to you if you don't listen to yourself first? But at some point it's time to share your intentions and help others with theirs.

What's Behind Your But

Sharing intentions is a risky business. Anyone you confide in can do whatever they like with them. They can lend support. They can steal the idea. Or they can thwart your plans. We'll see later how the challenge of sharing intentions is itself a master class in applying the Two But Rule.

For now, the point is that butting in on someone's shiny new intention requires a bit of care. You have to really understand what they want and why they want it. Consider this old chestnut, attributed to automotive pioneer Henry Ford: "If I had asked what my customers wanted, they would have said they wanted a faster horse."

The mistake most people make, when using this quote to justify why user input should be taken with a grain of salt, is focusing on the word *horse* and not on the word *faster*. There really was insight to be found in what customers wanted. They wanted to go faster. That said, focusing on *faster* doesn't necessarily get you to cars. One might have said, "But horses can't go faster, BUT maybe we could breed them for greater speed." That's a perfectly good pair of buts. However, it doesn't get you to the automobile or any other form of faster transportation.

There are a lot of reasons why someone would have wanted to go faster in 1903. To get their produce to market before it went bad. To get to and from distant work locations faster. To win races. But the mass adoption of Ford's Model T was driven by a new rural middle class eager to display its growing wealth and travel to leisure activities faster. These people wanted to show off. A faster horse wouldn't do.

These specific users, and their specific requirements, came with a new set of buts that produced a completely different product. This wasn't just about going from horses to cars. It was about the type of car.

If Ford had chosen the goal of winning early car races on closed, paved tracks, then the Model T would have been completely different. Instead, the important constraint was that in 1903 there was a lack of smooth paved roads in rural America. That led to Ford's historic second but: BUT we can make a car with big rubber tires and a lot of clearance to handle dirt roads.

Best Buy's Big Buts

While sharing intentions is risky, presenting your but in response to them is riskier. You have to consider several factors. Is the idea big enough to matter? Is it worth ruffling feathers and taking the conversation from passive assent to problem-solving? Is the idea articulated enough to signal that it's time to "but in"?

Daniel Garcia had one of those amazing "dumb" ideas that led to big results. Garcia was a Geek Squad Agent at big-box retailer Best Buy in Los Angeles, California, in the early days after the advent of the iPhone. He wanted customers who ordered home delivery and installation of appliances to see his car on an interactive map so that they would know he was on his way. He thought that seeing the car on the map would be better for the customer, because they'd get a sense of when to be ready for arrival. And he just thought it would be a fun thing to build.

At that time, Best Buy was running a program for employees that gave them nine weeks to prove a new concept or line of business. Garcia was accepted to the program and joined a team of three, including USC students Tal Flanchraych and Anthony Ko. The team quickly concluded that Geek Squad customers really didn't need or want the feature that Garcia was proposing—not enough to warrant the effort of building and managing the application…at least not in those days.

After a few weeks of exploring alternative ideas, the team went to a party. Many failed attempts to find a cab left them grumbling, and they returned home complaining about how they could never find a cab in Los Angeles. The geographic area of Los Angeles was so large compared to the number of taxis on the road that an available car might be right around the corner, but you wouldn't know it was there. And calling dispatch was a waste of time, especially on a Friday night.

The next day, they came up with a new idea. They imagined using a smartphone's GPS and cellular connectivity to transmit the locations of taxis and put them on users' smartphone screens. They spent the remainder of their nine weeks building a demo, which they called Cabulous after Flanchraych said, "Being able to see a taxi three blocks away and get it to pick me up would be cabulous."

This led to the founding of a new company that operates today as Flywheel, and it helped to inspire the ridesharing industry.

Here was their path from a little but to a big BUT:

1. "What if we put Geek Squad cars on a smartphone map?"
2. "But customers aren't interested."
3. "BUT we could use the same approach to end the era of the invisible taxi."

The Best Buy case illustrates how a relatively small idea led to a really big insight, one that helped shape the experience of getting a ride for hundreds of millions of people.

Uber's Bigger Buts

The Best Buy crew thought they had a big idea, but it turns out there was a bigger one. And it shows how picking powerful priorities is not done by simply asking people what they want and giving it to them, even if you're focused on why they want it. You also have to be clever about who you ask and how you hear them. Some people have more interesting reasons to want something than others.

In the field of product management, some product execs call the process of understanding what users really want "finding the *so that*":

User X wants Y so that Z.

A product requirement that says "The user needs a button" doesn't give a team much to work with. A more vivid requirement would say, "A person standing in the rain with a bag of groceries in one hand needs a button that's easy to push so that they can hail a taxi with their other hand." With this level of detail, design and engineering might even come back with a solution that's better than a button, because now they understand the situation and the goal.

The Best Buy team that created Flywheel built one of the first apps to track and hail taxis in 2008 on the assumption that users wanted to hail a ride *so that* they could get home from work or get to the airport. Their focus was on relieving the stress of wondering where the car was while they waited. Nothing wrong with that, but…

Then Uber arrived on the scene in 2010. On the surface, it might seem like they were targeting the same problem. However, at least by some accounts, Uber got its start by focusing on a different user, one with a different objective than simply getting a ride.

In 2010, smartphones were still new. A taxi booked with one of the new ride-hailing apps would show up only about 60 percent of the time, and usually late. This situation was bad enough for someone trying to get a ride to the airport. But it was a complete mismatch for a different kind of user: dudes—it was usually dudes—at a party or nightclub needing a convenient ride to "my place or yours."

Both the person on the way to the airport and *dude-at-a-party* wanted the same thing: to push a button and get a ride. But Dude wanted to pull a ride out of the air with a fancy new iPhone so that the subject of their amorous intentions might be impressed enough to go home with them. And a broken-down Crown Victoria taxi with gum stuck to the seats showing up late wasn't going to cut it.

All this left Uber with a new and different problem to solve, one that had little to do with the concerns of someone racing to the airport. Fortunately for Dude, there was another group with a problem of their own: limo drivers.

In 2010, cities like San Francisco maintained local ordinances preventing limousines from picking up random passengers off the street. Only taxis could do that. Limo passengers had to book their transportation with a dispatcher in advance over the phone.

There were reasons for this. Taxis were required to charge lower, regulated fares designed to make rides affordable for lower-income people. Also, taxi fleets were required to bear the cost of making a certain percentage of their cars wheelchair accessible. In exchange for this quasi-public/private partnership, cities restricted competition from limos, which had greater latitude in what they could charge. In San Francisco, the fine for a limo violating this rule and picking up random people off the street was $2,000 per incident.

Consequently, many limo drivers sat in their very nice cars idling in parking lots waiting for a call from their dispatchers. They wanted to fill that wasted time with paying customers, but they couldn't…BUT they could if Uber gave them a way to skirt the regulation and pick up rides in between their traditional bookings. Connecting limo drivers with dude-at-a-party was a match made in gig-economy heaven.

Today, Uber's main story is, "Get a Prius driven by some random guy for less than a taxi…usually." But in 2010, the story was, "Get a fancy limo for slightly more than a taxi and maybe get lucky in the process."

Uber quickly went from being a novelty for dude-at-a-party to handling a wide range of needs, including getting home from the grocery store and making it to the airport on time. But Dude was *patient zero*.

Patient zero is the most specific addressable target user that a new product can focus on. They are not the *only* user, not even the majority of early users. Patient zero is the user who will love the product so much that they will tell everyone about it. And the best patient zero is well connected to adjacent users who will also love the product with zero (or minimal) changes to its features.

So instead of working fruitlessly to get drivers of dilapidated taxis to show up consistently, Uber easily got fancy limo drivers, who were grateful for the work, to show up on time for a client base that was willing and able to pay a premium. That made it possible to provide an insanely great experience to people that could help the service go viral while minimizing early operating costs and enjoying higher revenue per ride.

This shows how the *so that*s of different patient zeros can lead to different buts, which can lead to entirely different results. If patient zero for Uber had been a low-income senior citizen in a wheelchair needing a ride home from the grocery store at a consistent, low price *so that* they could have self-sufficiency, all sorts of other issues—ones that cities have struggled with forever—would have risen to the top of Uber's early priority list. Even today, a ride-sharing industry that utilizes the practice of surge pricing is clearly not yet prioritizing these users. That could be the subject of a whole 2Buts story of its own.

Was Uber a paragon of awesomeness in 2010, or was it cherry-picking the ripest high-priced rides and leaving the rest to the struggling municipal taxi system? Either way you see it, you have to admit that Uber really knew how to pick its but.

5

Advanced Butology

So far we've been talking about different kinds of buts. We have 1Buts and 2Buts, which come in different sizes and shapes, including my favorite—the fuzzy but. We know what happens if we ignore our buts or end things on an odd-numbered but. And we've learned about the importance of intentions and listening for what's behind them. Now it's time to put it all together and get our buts ready for tackling complex issues, which I group into the very unscientific term *gnarly problems*.

Gnarly Buts

The Two But Rule can be applied to many kinds of issues, but it's especially useful when dealing with a gnarly problem—one where the thing that makes a problem persist, or the thing preventing you from achieving a goal, is also providing benefits you don't want to give up.

In the world of genetics, sickle cell anemia is a good example of this. It's a blood disorder that can cause organ damage, strokes, and reduced life expectancy. People with the condition tend to experience debilitating pain and fatigue. It's caused by a mutation in the human HBB gene, which provides instructions for making a protein in red blood cells essential for delivering oxygen throughout the body.

Typically, a mutation like this would get selected out of the gene pool, because individuals who have it are less likely to survive and reproduce—at least during the pre-technological age of human evolution. So we shouldn't see sickle cell anemia today. But we do. And the reason why is a good example of a gnarly problem.

Malaria is another terrible disease caused by parasites that infect humans through the bites of mosquitoes. It reproduces inside red blood cells and can cause seizures, respiratory distress, organ failure, and death. But blood cells with the sickle cell mutation disrupt the malaria parasite and increase survival rates. So as humans evolved in regions where malaria was endemic, the survival advantage provided by the sickle cell mutation outweighed the risk of having offspring with sickle cell anemia.

Today, of course, if we could snap our fingers and remove the HBB mutation entirely, we'd have better ways to manage malaria. At the time of this writing, Anthony James of the University of California, Irvine, has announced that they have used the gene editing technology CRISPR to take the genes from mice, whose immune systems can fight malaria, and put them into the genes of mosquitos. Introduced into the wild, these mosquitoes can breed quickly and become dominant in the population.

But, as Dana Perls of the nonprofit Friends of the Earth points out, the risks of releasing a bioengineered mosquito into the wild, one that can't be recalled, presents risks. We don't know what the consequences might be. This would be a good opportunity for James and folks like Perls to conduct a few healthy rounds of the Two But Rule.

Unfortunately, they are currently going for the old standby: digging into their positions and talking past each other. James simply says that he doesn't think there's much of a risk and is plowing ahead with plans to run tests out in nature, starting with a remote island. (Yeah…shades of *Jurassic Park*.) Perls is, for her part, also digging in, not embracing the intent of the professor's work but instead suggesting it should be scrapped in favor of other techniques she prefers, such as vaccines and general hygiene. Oh well. Clearly they haven't read this book…yet.

But even before the modern age, biology gave us its own 2But for sickle cell: symptoms of sickle cell anemia present when a child gets the HBB mutation from both the mother and the father. But if the child gets the mutation from only the mother or the father, symptoms largely don't appear or are mild. It's nature saying, "But we don't want what protects the population from malaria to make the entire population worse off, BUT we can limit the cases of serious illness to those who roll *snake eyes* in our genetic game of chance."

Scientists call this trick of natural selection *balanced polymorphism*. We might think of it as the "double-edged sword" problem. In economics, it pops up in theories about making decisions that involve trade-offs. Momentum Thinking is a way to find the optimal balance. And sometimes it's a way to see how a source of problems can be transformed into a source of benefits.

The next time you spot what seems like an unsolvable problem, an unacceptable trade-off, consider saying, "But we can't get rid of xyz without unacceptable consequences, BUT we could turn it into something less harmful and more useful if we…."

Chain of Buts

There are times when a single round of the Two But Rule will suffice. But most of the time, especially when tackling gnarly problems, a 2But is going to present new issues. It's not uncommon to go five or more rounds and cover not just one "But that won't work" but several in parallel. Life is a chain of buts and rarely just a single chain.

Building a chain of buts to overcome a complicated problem or capture a nuanced opportunity might look like this:

"We could do X."

"But that won't work, because A, B, and C."

"But A would work if D, B if E, and C if F."

"But F won't work, because G."

"But G would work if H."

...and so on.

The key is to make sure that when you add up each chain, the number is always divisible by 2.

To illustrate, let's look at the field of blockchain. There were more than 780 million people interacting with blockchains at the end of 2022. And with a trillion dollars of money held on them—much more or much less on any given day—the many problems with the technology and its uses (any one of which would normally be a showstopper) had become a square array of problems-to-solve.

For anyone just arriving from 2007, a *blockchain* is just a kind of database with a few special properties that make it interesting for recording transactions. Think of it as a digital bank ledger that won't allow anyone, even a system administrator, to do the following:

- Erase or change previously confirmed entries
- Falsely claim that a particular transaction didn't occur
- Censor or prohibit a valid transaction from being processed

It does this by allowing anyone to operate a copy of the ledger and collaborate to agree on the validity and ordering of the transactions. Sounds simple, right? It's not.

Here we could go into the many wonky details about blockchain technology, but in terms of Momentum Thinking the most important thing is this: the technology is less interesting than the intentions of the people using it.

The intentions of the people who launched the blockchain that popularized the concept of cryptocurrency—you may have heard of Bitcoin—were very specific: move money around the world directly from one person to another without the possibility of any government, bank, or other centralized organization being able to intervene or learn who is transacting.

When Bitcoin entered the scene in 2008, the world was grappling with the collapse of the banking industry, caused by historic levels of incompetence and greed. It was easy to appreciate Bitcoin's "crypto-anarchist" goals.

In the decade that followed, Bitcoin's growth went hyperbolic, with thousands of other blockchains springing up to copy or innovate on the design. Banks and big companies like IBM even tried to get in on the act. (Sadly, it turns out that a blockchain run by a set of known organizations misses the point of the technology and devolves into becoming just a more complicated, slow, and less secure version of a traditional database.)

The hype around the subject of blockchain and its associated buzzwords (terms like Web3, DeFi, NFTs, cryptocurrency, and tokens) exploded in the early 2020s. Were it not for this viral expansion—and the seductive power of buying a token and watching it grow hundreds or thousands of times in value almost overnight—the technical, regulatory, political, economic, and basic commonsense problems with blockchain technology might have brought it all down like a house of cards long before.

Here's how we might look at the industry's challenges from the perspective of Momentum Thinking:

1: The intention is to move money anonymously.

1.1: But every transaction is public. A public blockchain is essentially a digital nudist colony. And in today's world of advanced artificial intelligence, there's enough data out there for a growing number of actors to figure out who you are, what you have, and who you're transacting with.

Now applying our first 2But, we get the following:

1.2: BUT we can use new techniques such as zero knowledge cryptography to let people transact without any observer being able to know the accounts transacting or the amounts involved in the transactions. We can also use a system called a *mixer* to further confuse anyone trying to track money flows.

That sounds pretty good, but here comes a 3But:

1.3: But if we make cryptocurrencies truly private and untraceable, then bad guys get to launder money with impunity.

At the same time, here's a different intention:

2: The goal is to achieve a new form of digital money, free of government intervention and onerous banking fees.

2.1: But because blockchains like Bitcoin are designed to sacrifice scalability, speed, and efficiency for decentralization and censorship resistance, every transaction comes with a significant marginal cost. During times of network congestion, the transaction fee for the $2 pack of gum you want to buy with cryptocurrency can rise to hundreds of dollars.

2.2: BUT we don't have to run all the transactions directly on big public blockchains. A variety of approaches have been developed to enable more efficient machines to manage peer-to-peer transactions and then settle them in batches on a blockchain. The idea is to reduce the marginal cost of any given transaction.

2.3: But adding more layers of computing on top of blockchains leads to complexity, and complexity is the enemy of security. By 2022, the favorite way for scammers and thieves to steal billions in cryptocurrency was by exploiting flaws in the bridges between these systems.

Here's one more set of issues:

3: The goal is to bank the unbanked and foster financial inclusion for all.

3.1: But the nature of today's cryptocurrencies is such that people who acquired tokens early can become fabulously wealthy, driving up prices for essential goods and services, while latecomers tend to get wiped out in bubble crashes. Even if cryptocurrency prices stabilize, the descendants of people who didn't collect tokens early could become subjugated to the hegemonic power of the crypto-elites.

3.2: BUT we can design future cryptocurrencies to better ensure financial inclusion. We can enact policies, enforced by blockchain-based decentralized autonomous organizations (DAOs), to regularly drop tokens on community members' accounts so that they don't get left behind.

3.3: But anonymous users voting to reduce the purchasing power of their hoarded wealth to level the playing field for newcomers seems like a dubious proposition.

And so on.

For each of these buts, there's another but being theorized, proposed, or deployed. Telling the full story of all the pairs of buts at play in blockchain could fill a five-year Netflix series.

The ultimate second but for blockchain is clear. The money and power involved here is astronomical, beyond the dreams of avarice. There are a ton of ultra-rich people for whom blockchain provides an excellent fit for their needs: the ability to move large fistfuls of money across borders relatively untraceably. Because of the huge amount of money to be made on cryptocurrency—practically out of thin air—many of the best minds in the world have been drawn into the effort of figuring it out.

You'll notice that I ended this story on three odd-numbered buts. As I said, I recently experienced an interruption in my supply of buts on this topic. And so, the next 2Buts are for others to find. But as I hope you'll see by the end of the book, there is always hope, even in the 1Buts we leave behind. And it's worth mentioning that as I wrote this book, I found a few new buts to consider—at least a few ways to get the benefits of the industry's advanced cryptography research. But let's move on.

We'll see later how powerful it is to explore issues through several parallel rounds of the Two But Rule. And we'll cover a variety of new tools to help manage the process. But the point of Momentum Thinking isn't to prescribe a rigid framework. It's enough to be lightly aware of the pattern as you go through life. That subtle habit of being mindful of your many buts can be life-changing. And when you find yourself lost in an endeavor that seems hopelessly mired in problems, groupthink, and gridlock, your ability to string together a chain of buts and stick with it when others give up can be a powerful source of insight, comfort, and momentum.

Rediscovering Your But

Speaking of revisiting old 1Buts, let's talk about the cycles of science. Thomas Kuhn's 1962 book *The Structure of Scientific Revolutions* is one of the most cited academic books of all time. It's also a good guide to Momentum Thinking.

Revolutionary inflection points in scientific knowledge, according to Kuhn, are different from normal periods of scientific progress. Paradigm shifts, like the move from Newton's classical physics to Einstein's theory of relativity, deliver new ways of explaining the world and new tools to solve old problems...and sometimes to find new ones.

These are important moments to revisit old buts and see if any new buts appear, any new ways to achieve momentum. For example, a munitions engineer in 1890 might have said, "We want to blow up a whole city with one bomb, but we can't."

Compare that to what someone on the Manhattan Project might have said in 1942: "We still can't blow up a whole city, BUT we could if we used atomic fission."

Admittedly not the most inspiring case, but it illustrates the point. New tools, particularly during shifts in scientific theory, can lead to an explosion of new answers to old problems. And, as this case also illustrates, new buts tend to appear: "But after we blow up the enemy's city, radiation can blow over us."

It's true. Rather than reducing the field of problems and solutions, the Two But Rule, combined with scientific progress, tends to expand it—like mushrooms...or mushroom clouds.

It used to be that scientific revolutionaries, and innovators in general, had a tough time convincing the establishment to break with the past and adopt their new ideas. Today, we seem to have the opposite problem. It's hard for established practices that still work well to get any attention against the background noise of innovation mania.

The irony of today's infatuation with "disruptive innovation" is that we're casting old buts as new ones without the benefit of any actual advancement in scientific knowledge to warrant it. The world has become a "JJ Abrams reboot" of everything, and as in some of his movies, flashy lens flares hide real flaws in the story.

On the other hand, important advances don't have to come from scientific revolutions. Recently, radical improvements in the relatively old field of artificial intelligence are delivering new 2Buts to old 1Buts in a key area of life sciences that has stymied researchers for decades.

Proteins Got a Brand New But

There are at least 200 million different proteins that form the basis of all life. Proteins are tiny—about two nanometers on average—made from the same kinds of amino acid building blocks as DNA. If DNA is the architect of everything you are, proteins make up most of the building and run everything from the security cameras to the air conditioning.

Proteins spontaneously fold into three-dimensional shapes, and they do this in a couple milliseconds. There are so many ways they can fold that to model them all would take most advanced computers about the same amount of time as the current age of the universe to run the calculations.

And there's the problem. Characterizing proteins, understanding their shapes and the way the shapes change as they fold, is essential for understanding and curing disease. But the size, speed, and variation involved make it incredibly difficult to characterize them. Techniques such as X-ray crystallography are time-consuming, costly, and maddeningly finicky. And because of this, by 2019 fewer than 1 percent of known proteins had been characterized.

In the early 2000s, computer companies offered a second but: "We can't easily see or characterize proteins, BUT we can make massive supercomputers that might be able to model how they fold. By 2007, IBM's Blue Gene supercomputer, named for its intended purpose of modeling protein folding, became the fastest such machine in the world. By 2018, it could reach 20 petaflops per second, an astronomical figure for the time. And yet, while it went on to great success in many other fields, it produced few results in protein folding. Trying to crack the folding problem with the brute force of faster computers was, according to one commentator, a catastrophic failure.

Today, projects like Blue Gene are shuttered, and computer modeling has become the old but: "But the fastest computer we can build still can't approach the 10^300 permutations needed to model protein folding. To carry on with the brute-force approach, we'll need to wait for quantum computers, and that's still far in the future."

BUT, in 2018 a project called AlphaFold used artificial intelligence to win a long-running annual protein characterization competition. It won again in 2020, garnering general praise as a once-in-a-generation advancement. And in 2022, the team released folding models for nearly all 200 million known proteins. And they did it with conventional computers, not supercomputers like Blue Gene.

The *Guardian* reported in July 2022 that scientists were already using some of AlphaFold's predictions to help develop new medicines.

So, the old 1But, "We wanted to model proteins, but the problem was too big for our most advanced supercomputers," found a new 2But, "BUT we could change the approach and use artificial intelligence (AI)."

What's notable about this is that most of these AI techniques have been around for decades. The new 2But didn't come from a new scientific revolution. Instead, it came from radical improvements to an old one.

New buts can appear out of the blue, when you least expect them. So in addition to regularly scanning old problems for new solutions when new scientific paradigms appear, don't forget to keep an eye out for conventional improvements to existing tools that allow them to change the game.

Hidden Buts

One of the most advanced topics in butology is spotting hidden intentions and objections. Some hide in plain sight. For example, if you've ever been an entrepreneur or small business owner, you know how hard it can be to rationally consider doing something new or different, or even doing what you're already doing *differently*. You're one pay cycle from going out of business, one false move from getting run over by the competitor, or one bad meeting from getting thrown out by your board of directors. Your hidden intention is to avoid having to contemplate change. When someone says "But you have this issue, BUT you could solve it by...," you have your own 1But: "But please go away. I'll think about new things when I'm done with my current *new thing*."

If, on the other hand, you want to get anywhere with your suggestion to an entrepreneur or small business, you're going to need to have thought through the following special pair of buts beforehand: "But this person isn't going to listen to my idea, because they are up all night, every night, just keeping the lights on. BUT I could make this idea feel boring and simple and slip it into their operation without triggering their innovation gag reflex if I...."

Another example of a hidden intention is one that simply isn't there but ought to be. In 1494, Spain and Portugal signed the Treaty of Tordesillas in what might seem like a clever application of the Two But Rule. The treaty was meant to handle a conflict over newly discovered territories, dividing lands outside Europe along a meridian about 1,000 miles west of the Cape Verde Islands. Lands to the west would belong to Portugal, and lands to the east would belong to Spain. Each side had several objections. They were worked out, and the treaty was signed. But, while each side's intentions and objections were neatly squared by the treaty, there was a glaring omission. The interests and intentions of the people already living in those newly discovered lands—and lands yet to be discovered—were absent from any consideration in the negotiations.

While this is unsurprising given the times and the players involved, we can do better today. We can remember to add a but. "But who else will our decisions negatively impact?" We might answer, "We don't know, but we could find out if we...." And if there are other interests discovered, then the Two But Rule can be applied again to square the original intentions, honor the objections (including the newly discovered negative impacts), and then try to square them to meet everyone's needs.

If, on the other hand, the answer to the discovery of potential harms to others is, "But we don't care about them," then, well, it's a good thing we've come to the part of this book that deals with "bad buts."

6

Bad Buts

The Two But Rule isn't a panacea, and it's not a technique you can unthinkingly apply to any situation. There's a subtle art to it. It comes from understanding that what people want is never as interesting or as important as why they want it. It's essential to honor those intentions and not disregard them, even if you disagree. Without that, you can wind up with something like this: "But that's a dumb idea, BUT it wouldn't be if you threw it out and went with my idea instead."

Or your colleague might say, "Let's go left," and you then say, "*But* I don't want to go left, BUT we could go right instead!"

This doesn't help with momentum, though it is useful…in a way. The 1But doesn't tell your colleague much, just that you're opposed to going left. The 2But, at least, reveals your own intention. Now you both know that you aim to go in opposite directions. There's some utility in that. You've achieved awareness and transparency. You had a secret intention hiding in your but, and your 2But but revealed it. Good for you!

And yet, using your but this way too often will reduce the practice to a sterile technique, like wordplay without impact. It won't help you solve problems, establish rapport, and build innovative momentum.

A well-crafted but seeks to find some way to understand and advance the intentions of the other person...without glossing over your own intentions or concerns. Even a silly or fuzzy 2But that reflects the original idea can let the person know at least that they were heard: "BUT we could go both right and left together at the same time, if we grew really long legs, locked arms, and took a huge step left and then a huge step right." Will that get you somewhere? Maybe not. But it shows you're committed to doing whatever you're going to do together.

On the other hand, a second but that doesn't reflect the original intent will reveal that you weren't listening or didn't care enough to show that you were. After too much of this, the positivity police will take charge again and enforce a no-buts policy on the team, killing momentum in the process.

How does this work with real people in real situations? Here's a true story of a team applying the Two But Rule the right way when they literally encountered a fork in the river.

Lewis and Clark's Historic Buts

On June 3, 1805, the Lewis and Clark expedition, which had been commissioned by Thomas Jefferson to find a water passage across North America to the Pacific Ocean, ran into a problem.

They had come to the junction of two large rivers, one feeding into the Missouri River from the north, and one from the south. Their orders were to explore the Missouri to its headwaters, and Native American guides had given them good directions on how to get there. Until now. They had no information on this fork, and they couldn't readily determine which was the continuation of the Missouri.

The team made observations to determine which fork would take them to the headwaters and into the Rocky Mountains. Nearly everyone believed the correct course was to the north, but Lewis and Clark believed the south fork was the right one.

They were in charge, so they could have simply said, "You all want to go north, but we don't think that's right, BUT we could go south."

Instead, they sent a scouting party up each fork about 10 miles. Both parties returned with no conclusive observations to suggest which was the right choice. Then they led parties further up both forks, with Lewis covering more than 60 miles. Still no conclusive evidence. Except that now even their most expert waterman, Private Cruzatte, was convinced that the north fork was the Missouri.

At this point, the captains made the decision to go against the advice of the crew and take the south fork, but they made preparations that would minimize the time lost if they were wrong.

Lewis wrote in his journal on June 9, before heading south: "In the evening Cruzatte gave us some music on the violin and the men passed the evening in dancing singing…and were extreemely cheerfull (sic)." In the end, the south fork was the right choice.

So to recap, on June 3 the team wanted to go north, but the captains wanted to go south, BUT they chose to conduct two brief scouting missions. (Notably, this led to Lewis discovering two birds previously unknown to science, which nicely illustrates the unexpected fruits of the Two But Rule.) Then, even after choosing the south fork, they effectively said, "BUT if we're wrong, we'll send a fast team overland and shorten the time needed to double back, if necessary."

It's an extraordinary example of leadership and teamwork. The captains went against the choice of nearly the entire crew, including their expert on the subject. Because they showed that they were listening and taking actions to collect the best information they could—and because of well-earned trust and camaraderie that had already been established in the team—the crew didn't resort to grudging compliance. Apparently they had a party instead.

In moments like this, the key is to focus on the long game, the higher intention, the why behind the immediate intention. This wasn't a contest between two separate intentions, one to go north and the other to go south. On the contrary, everyone in the expedition had the same goal. Make it to the Pacific.

Intentions matter in maintaining momentum. The intention of the positivity police is to get along. The intention of 1But-guy is, among other things, to exercise a compulsion. Neither is motivated by maintaining forward momentum. The intention of the Lewis and Clark expedition? Make the best choice possible, under conditions of uncertainty, but keep moving. Winter was coming.

It's no good to use Momentum Thinking as a way of rejecting an idea and doubling down on your own intentions. But you can also swing the other way and find yourself hunting for a second but to solve your objection to somebody's terrible idea and wind up reinforcing an unworthy premise.

If someone said, "I want to stick this pencil in your eye," an incorrect application of the Two But Rule would be to say, "But that would be hard to do, BUT it wouldn't be, if…."

In a case like this, you want to back up and figure out what's behind the other person's intention. For example, you could say, "But I don't want you to stick that pencil in my eye, BUT I can see why you want to. So a) I'm sorry; and b) You can punch me in the arm if it helps."

The key is to honor their real needs, not necessarily the specific thing they proposed. Keeping a keen eye on human needs behind the points and counterpoints of an argument, the ideas and issues of a brainstorming session, or the objectives and obstacles of a planning meeting will help you discover paths to better outcomes and avoid tangents, dead ends, and distractions.

Cheating Buts

Many zealots, charlatans, con artists, and world leaders have shown absolute mastery of the Two But Rule while using it for nefarious (or at least self-serving) intentions. When they hear "But your evil plan won't work…," they respond with "BUT it would if…."

Any professional con artist knows the value of the Two But Rule. When presented with something seemingly impossible in the physical universe we occupy, there is always the option for sleight of hand. For examples of this, I direct you to a range of enjoyable movie selections: *Ocean's 11, The Sting, Now You See Me*, and *Catch Me If You Can*.

And this isn't just an enticing choice for crooks. It's a lesson *Star Trek*'s Captain Kirk applied when faced with the dreaded Kobayashi Maru test, an ordeal designed to present a captain with a no-win scenario to teach a lesson about facing failure and death. Kirk's answer? "BUT we could cheat." That is what he did in multiple reboots of the *Star Trek* franchise, secretly reprogramming the test to allow him to beat it. Even when presented with a powerful second but—"But if you cheat death, you will not learn to face it"—a handy plot device provides Kirk with another but: BUT he can learn to face death by watching his friend Spock die…and later we can bring Spock back to life. Win-win.

That's how it works in the movies. In the real world, the "BUT we could cheat" option usually represents a failure to think a problem through, or at least a failure to think laterally. Volkswagen learned this the hard way.

Volkswagen's Gassy But

Between 2005 and 2007, the United States announced stringent new automobile emissions standards. These required that by 2010 diesel vehicles had to reduce nitrogen oxide (NOx) emissions by 93 percent, from 1 gram per mile to .07 grams. At the same time, Volkswagen was eagerly expanding into the U.S. market with diesel vehicles. There were technical solutions that would allow diesel engines to comply with the standard, but each came with compromises.

For example, selective catalytic reduction technology used a urea solution to break down NOx into nitrogen and water, but it required extra space for the tank holding the urea, and customers had to refill it periodically. Asking customers to bear the cost and trouble of filling their car *essentially with pee* does seem like a legitimate concern.

Volkswagen chose a different solution called a lean NOx trap (LNT). This had its own trade-offs, and chief among them was that Volkswagen engineers couldn't find a way to make it reduce emissions enough to comply with the standard. BUT...yeah, they could cheat.

Between 2009 and 2015, Volkswagen sold roughly 500,000 diesel cars in the United States, claiming that they met the standard thanks to innovative engineering. And that was true. The innovation, however, wasn't in finding a way to make LNTs work. It was in figuring out a way to detect when the car was going through emissions tests and set the LNT to minimize pollutants, while emitting 40 times the legal limit under normal driving conditions.

Volkswagen applied the laziest form of the Two But Rule: "But we can't meet the standard, BUT we could fool the test." If they had bothered to do more than one round of Momentum Thinking, they might have concluded what manufacturers like Mercedes Benz already had: "But getting caught is very likely (3But), BUT we can combine several technologies to comply with the standard while minimizing customer inconvenience (4But)."

As it turned out, Mercedes Benz and others discovered that U.S. customers buying diesel were environmentally conscious, so the additional emissions devices were a selling point. Mercedes saw strong sales in the years after implementing the changes.

Volkswagen's deception came to light in September 2015 and had massive impacts on the company's finances and market reputation. They posted a $1.8 billion loss in 2016, the first loss in 20 years. They had to cover billions in fines and vehicle buybacks. CEO Martin Winterkorn resigned, and one executive went to jail.

The challenges Volkswagen faced in complying with the new standard were formidable. Technical solutions didn't materialize, not ones that didn't involve what management considered to be unacceptable trade-offs. If they had, it would have been a simple round of the Two But Rule: "We have to comply with the new standard, BUT we can use our new magic diesel catalytic converter that is cheaper, reduces fuel consumption, makes the car go faster, and gives the air around it a minty fresh scent."

Gnarly problems like this require not only a mastery of running multiple rounds of Momentum Thinking but managing multiple dimensions of it so that solutions can present themselves across different lateral lines of thought. That's what allowed other manufacturers to take a different path. They said,

"But it will cost more, BUT we have customers who will pay for it, if they understand how it aligns with their values."

Don't Be a Lazy But

Businesses commit crimes all the time. Often, they don't even know it. And when it comes to businesses based on emerging technology, it's such a big hazard that the playbook in recent years has become, "Ignore the law, move fast, raise a ton of money, and build a huge popular following. Then throw an army of lawyers at regulators after they belatedly wake up to your violations." In the early 2000s, this approach was disastrous for peer-to-peer file sharing companies, which got clobbered by the entertainment industry and law enforcement. Remember Napster? But the approach worked reasonably well for some gig economy businesses.

More recently, it seems like law enforcement is starting to get a handle on this game and is making it harder to play. Good. It's such a lazy game that it makes pickleball look like an Olympic sport. (Apologies to pickleball. Just know that if you love pickleball, you are 10x less of a lazy thinker than those entrepreneurs who partied themselves into cozy connections with venture capitalists looking to make a quick buck on regulatory arbitrage.)

Don't Argue with Your But

We've seen how the Two But Rule can be misunderstood, misused, overused, and outright abused. But the real tragedy is how seldom it's used at all. It's not yet remotely part of our common habit—not in our daily lives, not among the cognoscenti of Silicon Valley, not in academia, and certainly not in the halls of government.

Instead, we typically practice the adversarial method that you might have learned in high-school debate club. (Is debate club still a thing?) Someone presents an issue and proposes a solution. Then an opponent goes to work tearing it down. The first person then tries to prop up their original points, followed by the opponent tearing them down again.

There's utility in debate. It's a way to expose weak arguments. It's rigorous. And it's deeply human. But it falls short, particularly on problems where it appears as though the only way to get one thing is to give up another.

If you watch shows that pit talking heads against each other on thorny problems facing society, keep a tally of whether an argument comes to rest on an even- or odd-numbered but. It usually comes out odd, and at that point, you'll spot a moment where everyone begins repeating the position they'd already stated. They'll circle the drain, saying things like, "I heard you, but I still think…."

When an argument goes circular, you know they're stuck on an odd-numbered but, and they have lost touch with each other's intentions. After everyone is exhausted talking past each other, the debate often leads to an unnecessary game of winners and losers. The powerful say, "Here's what we're going to do." The opposition says, "But we don't want that." And the powerful respond, "BUT we're doing it anyway."

In other cases of 1Butism, people say things like, "We're in violent agreement." This is another trap. The combatants in a debate finally agreeing can feel satisfying, and certainly it's possible for a debate to uncover a solution that both sides can agree on. But sometimes this is a path to groupthink. Just because we have agreement doesn't mean we've arrived at the best outcome. It's possible, in fact, that we've simply combined the worst ideas from both sides and called it compromise.

The best objective of Momentum Thinking isn't compromise. It's finding the unexpected, innovative path to meeting everyone's needs. You use the Two But Rule to honor the original intention, honor all the objections, and then find a way to square all sides. True innovation is about taking a problem that looks like a seesaw, where you're up only if your friend is down, and turning that seesaw into an airplane wing that takes you both up together.

There's no question that there's a lot of value in using Momentum Thinking to open up our own thinking. But in the end, if we're going to turn a seesaw into an airplane wing, we're going to need to work together and manage the dynamics involved when we start presenting our buts in a social context.

2

The Two But Rule
in Practice

7

The Social Life of Buts

Momentum Thinking is a lot easier with help from other humans. They're in a much better position to see your but clearly. However, revealing your intentions to a room full of people who are likely to turn around and unceremoniously present their buts to you is like attending the Burning Man festival in the Nevada desert wearing nothing but body paint. At the very least, it takes some getting used to.

When it comes to applying the Two But Rule in a group, there are nuanced social dynamics at play, especially in a world where there are no buts allowed. These dynamics are at play when working in small groups, single companies, large distributed teams, and, as in the following case, when trying to work with teams across legally separate organizations.

Drunken Buts

The research departments of two companies—one in material science and the other in healthcare—met for a week to share their research into very small things—nanotech and cellular biology.

Day one began with the first company's chief scientist presenting a set of slides. In the afternoon, the second company's chief scientist followed suit. An attendee, bored to tears and finding solace in furtively opening his laptop and surfing the Web, noticed that in both cases the slides had been pulled from the companies' public websites.

What made the presentations that first day so boring was not simply that anyone could have read them on the Web and saved themselves the trouble of attending the conference. It was that the presentations were inert. The first scientist: "We're focusing on dendrimers and nanopores."

Followed by the second scientist: "We're focused on cytokine signaling and gene sequencing."

Aside from the technobabble, neither presented intentions. No problems to solve. No opportunities to capture. And definitely no signal of what might be standing between them and achieving their objectives. There was nothing to latch onto.

Here were two leaders, whose legal teams had spent months hammering out agreements that were supposed to make it safe to share confidential details about their work, getting nowhere, sharing nothing new.

One of the scientists in the audience turned to the organizer at the end of the day and whispered, "We brought the wrong people. We should have brought the interns." So the next day, at the prompting of the organizer, each company brought more junior scientists and interns to the event. Again, the day's presentations droned on, joylessly sharing nothing new, generating no sparks. But that night, after the senior scientists went to bed, the interns went to a local bar and got drunk.

By all accounts, the scene at the bar was raucous…at least by nerd standards. Excited discussions sprang up between tables. Grievances about lack of resources and support were voiced candidly. Arguments broke out. Buts rose into the air like flying monkeys. And in the days that followed, no fewer than five joint research projects were proposed on the floor of the general session.

During their breakouts and in the setting of the bar, they were able to share things with each other more deeply. And this had the side benefit of granting plausible deniability to senior managers in cases when someone might have shared too much.

Years later, it turns out they were onto something. Combining nanopore technology and gene sequencing led to a breakthrough that made possible the rapid sequencing of SARS COV-2 during the global pandemic of 2020, even in remote areas with limited resources. A quarter of all variant COVID genomes have been sequenced in this way, improving the chances of catching new strains wherever they appear. See what you can achieve when you rub your buts together across very different fields of study?

The Gaps in Your But

Whether lubricated by alcohol or well established and carefully fostered mutual trust, it's essential to reveal what you intend to do as well as what's thwarting your ability to achieve it. Likewise, you need people around you who will tell you both what they think won't work and how they might solve those issues.

The gap between what you want to do and what you can do might be technical: you might not know how to do something, what solutions could be applied, or why the solutions you have tried aren't working. We call this the know *how/what/why problem*.

Or the gap might be organizational: you want to work on one problem that fascinates you, but your boss wants you to work on something else. Or you don't have a connection to people who are able to support your intention, care about its goals, and trust you to be the one to make it happen if they support you.

Or the gap could be logical: the story or the initial work on the idea simply isn't showing enough value to prioritize further work over other options. This is the gap that leads to commercial failures even if the technology is good.

Usually, the gaps facing any good intention include examples of all three, and if you close all three of these gaps, you'll find that you won't have a resource or funding gap. If you've actually found a cure for cancer that doesn't kill the patient, require moon dust, or involve some other unacceptable trade-off, and if you can get the message to the right people who will believe you, then you won't have a problem getting resources. In fact, if it does require moon dust, you'll have a rocket waiting for you on the pad by the weekend.

Being willing to share your intentions and your gaps allows you to communicate your 1But to someone who might be able to help. Here's a super-nerdy example: "We think we could use nanopore materials to do gene sequencing without the time and expensive gear involved in existing PCR techniques, but we can't seem to get the translocation velocity right."

This allows your colleague to say: "Oh! That would be a big issue, BUT we figured out how to conjugate a moiety with a nucleic acid sequence that should help with the velocity problem."

If you ignore the only-somewhat-made-up technobabble and keep your eye on the buts in that conversation, you'll notice momentum building and a solution forming.

Exposing Your But

We need to share information across different organizations so that we can work together better in an increasingly complex and interconnected world—a world where what any of us does or knows can affect everyone else.

But, we can't share—not everything and not all the time—because some information is personal, sensitive, and confidential. We have legal, ethical, and practical reasons to protect it from leaks, misappropriation, and misalignment.

So we can't simply copy and send our most sensitive internal data to others, not even to our most trusted partners—not even when it would make everything we do together faster, smoother, and less expensive.

You can't throw a stick in any direction without hitting the "we need to share but can't share" problem. You experienced it the day you discovered your first crush. You needed help. Surely your friend could get the friend of your newfound love interest to assist in the dangerous courtship maneuver. Maybe they could orchestrate a way to seat you next to each other at a movie. But…so many buts. Your friend, you'll remember, had a big mouth. They could blab and ruin the whole affair. And you couldn't be sure they weren't interested in the same person—or that they would become interested, if they learned that you were.

Teenage courtships are a good illustration of the problem with sharing intentions. You need to know, before sharing, what your prospective confidante's intentions are, and you have to consider how their intentions might change once they become aware of yours. That's why, to this day, your blood pressure probably rises when remembering the first time you confided in someone like that.

Companies, governments, and pretty much any assemblage of humans interacting with any other assemblage of humans deal with this problem all day, every day. It's so pervasive that most of us are numb to it. And yet, if you're a CEO, I bet that thinking about the last time you had to reveal your plans to another company in order to achieve a mutual objective jacks your blood pressure higher than remembering your first crush.

Here are just a few examples of the dilemma:

Example 1: Ride-sharing apps, like many multisided markets, must connect people without violating their trust or putting them at risk by mishandling information about who they are, where they are, or where they're going. This gets even thornier when the applications making these connections involve dozens of third-party services like Google Maps and Twilio that sometimes need to orchestrate by passing customer data between them.

Example 2: Supply chains and logistics networks function better when each counterparty knows more about what the other is doing. But the more data counterparties have about each other, the greater the risk of that information getting into the hands of bad actors and competitors. Consequently, attempts to collect that information have met intractable resistance from vendors and nations repeatedly throughout modern history. Supply chain management will remain balkanized and brittle until a way to square the "we need to share but can't share" issue has been found and adopted.

Example 3: Imagine what we might discover if the world's R&D labs could share everything about what they're learning with each other, particularly if they could effectively absorb and act on that shared knowledge. But in the earliest phases of research and development, it's difficult to see clearly where the work will take you and how your intentions about what to do with it will change. Consequently, working out joint R&D contracts is a tricky business. And for every joint project, there are innumerable projects that never happened, simply because the parties never knew they should be working together.

It's essential to bridge the divide between teams and find opportunities to work together. But once we have everyone in the same room, the question becomes *how* we work together. That's what we'll cover next.

CHAPTER

8

Playing with Your But

In an accelerating world, one of the hardest things to do is spend real time playing with problems. As comedian John Cleese pointed out frequently in his decades-long side gig as a business innovation guru, creative people are prepared to tolerate the long periods of the discomfort we all experience when we haven't yet solved a problem. They're willing to play with it much longer before trying to resolve it.

Playing with our buts involves recognizing that what we're imagining won't work in the real world. That's the point of exploring it within the boundaries of play. And during this exploration, we allow both the fuzzy, illogical ideas and the silly, illogical buts that naturally arise to mingle and play together.

This creative juxtaposition is an essential ingredient in problem-solving, innovation, and comedy. Without it, you might have fun during playtime, but you're less likely to have something interesting when it's over. It's one thing to daydream about a world run by wizards. It's another to write a book that reconciles how such a world could coexist with the one we live in. Harry Potter *wouldn't be a very good book without the magic of buts.*

Taking time to play with unresolved problems and unrealized ideas is hard even for a single person, but it's especially tricky for teams. And it's impossible for teams that don't know how to have fun. Groups crumble under the anxiety of staying open about a hard problem when they don't have common experience, common space, and a common sense of humor.

It's no surprise that John Cleese, a comedian famous for his ensemble work with *Monty Python*, says we need teams that know how to relax and play together. He points out that if there's just one person in the group that makes you feel defensive, "Goodbye, creativity."

This is really important when it comes to applying the Two But Rule. It takes a lot of trust and amity to be able to say, "But I don't like that idea…." And if your team hasn't built up enough common experience to know that you will faithfully add "BUT I would like it if…," defensiveness surely will come. If there is no shared experience of fun, no common sense of humor, then it's game over. The positivity police will be on the scene before you can utter your second but.

The reason we must build a wider society of people who can laugh through their buts is obvious. Like humor, the best applications of the Two But Rule come when you connect two different mental frameworks together. Whether to tell a joke or solve a gnarly problem, juxtaposition is a powerful tool, and it happens to flow naturally from the practice of a diverse team that knows how to play together.

This has always been a tall order for teams, particularly diverse and geographically dispersed ones. But it has grown incredibly challenging in the world we live in now. The pandemic shaped a new reality where self-imposed work-from-home isolation became the norm even after the threat of COVID passed.

It's harder these days to have that chance encounter with a friend or colleague where you say, "You know what would be awesome to do?" and they say, "Well sure, but what about this problem?" at which point you both say, "But we could solve that problem by…."

Isolation is having an effect not only on spontaneity but on humor. These days, attempts at humor can carry a high risk of causing offense. What makes us laugh is often the unexpected twist, the irreverent quip, the flirtation with taboo. These can come to mind and leave the lips with little chance to catch them before they fall into a minefield of legitimately raw nerves, causing lasting harm to relationships.

That doesn't mean we should give up trying to find a way to laugh together. And it also doesn't mean we should return to the days of countenancing truly ugly schoolyard behavior in the name of "lightening up." If that sort of thing was ever truly funny, it isn't now.

Even among people who have returned to the office, there's a lingering, pervasive emotional distance. Some report fewer after-work gatherings, fewer informal conversations, and less laughter. And the remaining opportunities to build rapport and camaraderie are still lost for remote co-workers. An "us versus them" mentality under these conditions is hard to avoid. And there is nothing funny about that.

Fortunately, it's not impossible to establish rapport with remote teammates online. Digitally enhanced experiences can even present some advantages. The human brain is incredibly adaptable, and many people already claim to be more at home sharing ideas—and even being funny—through the medium of their phones, keyboards, and screens than being physically in the same room with others.

There are definitely trade-offs involved with remote teams, and so far digital collaboration tools have limited ways of achieving the natural spontaneity of an ad hoc physical encounter. But for the generations rising in the workforce today, living with those trade-offs is already the new normal.

Timing Your But

Squeezing your but into a team environment requires that everyone make room for it. That can be hard to do when everyone is talking over each other. And in a world of remote and hybrid work, finding ways to make time and space for everyone's buts is a subject worth studying. A few years ago, we did just that with a design company called IDEO.

IDEO is an icon in the design world. They had a hand in thousands of projects ranging from Apple's first usable computer mouse to the design of entire business models in retail and banking. Founder David Kelley significantly advanced the field of design thinking, which has led to generations of new product designers applying the IDEO method to everything from consumer products to climate change.

In the early 2000s, IDEO was engaged by a research lab to conduct a day of design sessions with a team of 50 MBAs, scientists, and software developers. Normally, IDEO is the one conducting experiments, but unbeknownst to them, this was an experiment on IDEO itself. The intention was to test the effectiveness of face-to-face ideation sessions against remote sessions.

The experiment involved three sessions. The first was an in-person event of structured, facilitated brainstorming. The second was conducted on a conference call, with all 50 people calling in from their own phones. The third was run via chat software, with everyone remotely logged in and typing in a single chat room.

The first event was enjoyable. IDEO really knows how to run a room. It produced one new idea that led to a patent filing. (Patents are by no means the best measure of innovation, but at least you can count them.)

The second event, as you might expect, was a living mess. Fifty people were on a call, and the moderators were barely able to keep people from talking over each other. When they did get things under control, most of the participants had mentally checked out.

The third event was a new experience for the team. The age of teams constantly chatting on Slack and Discord was still 15 years away. There were concerns that a single-threaded chat room (which was all that the technology supported then) would lead to an incoherent jumble of confused conversations. But instead, the team somehow navigated the many threads of conversation, and in the end, a half-dozen ideas came out. Roughly five of them led to patent filings.

The experiment, however, was not about innovation, ideas, or even patents. The experiment was about the effects of blocking.

Different humans are wired differently when it comes to conversational timing. Culture, brain diversity, and personal habit all play a role in how swiftly one speaks, how often one speaks up, how long one grandstands before pausing, and how long one waits to speak after someone else has finished speaking.

Timing mismatches on teams lead to both practical and social problems. Within the context of a relatively slow-talking culture, a fast-talker who interjects something a few seconds before the previous speaker stops talking can be annoying to others. They might find it inappropriate or an indication that the speaker wasn't listening. On the other hand, in a room of fast-talkers who are comfortable talking over each other in a coffee-powered frenzy, a slow-talker can be seen as disinterested or as a free-rider.

Differences in timing lead to blocking. Some people get more floor time and others less. In the live, face-to-face session, blocking was held in check by physical cues and the skilled IDEO moderator's ability to see who wanted to speak but didn't want to interrupt. This led to a larger number of people speaking. Still, there were people who never said a thing and others who seemed never to stop talking.

The moderators were flummoxed by the conference call. They had no visual cues to work with, and there were no side conversations. This led not only to dismal results but serious negative feelings, which had to be managed later as people counted their grievances.

The third event, being over text chat, involved no visual cues and no way to sense someone else's tone of voice. It was just a stream of text. There was literally no blocking. People who had never contributed to a conversation became virtual chatterboxes. And the traditional fast-talkers later recounted feeling better, because they weren't sensing the ambient disdain from people they had blocked in face-to-face meetings.

One observer of the experiment noted that the absence of both visual and audio cues actually helped with participation. Age, physical presence, intonation, and other factors fell away. Even rank, which the contributors still were aware of as they responded to others, became less of a factor in limiting or altering what they said. While this might not be the way to conduct a social gathering, it appears to have benefits when it comes to collaborating on ideas.

Butting In

If you have a habit of butting in too quickly in conversations, Momentum Thinking offers a useful antidote. Formulate your 2But before you articulate your 1But. It will help you smooth out your conversational pacing, reduce the chance of 1Butism or *yeah-butting* making you appear oppositional, and the act of mentally seeking the 2But will help you hold your thought and not forget what you want to say.

For some, the fear of losing track of their thought as the conversation trundles along is what drives the urge to hop in quickly with a yeah-but, whatabout, or other form of 1Butism. Seeking the second but cements the thought, connects it, and if it's worth the team's time, it usually finds its way back into the conversation. Your idea will not be, as *Blade Runner*'s Roy Beatty said, "Lost in time, like tears in rain." Fear not. Try it for yourself.

The Odious But

Whether due to long exposure to the blocking problem or other factors that lead to damaged relationships, there are times when you're going to be presented with a perfectly good pair of buts by people you don't like, respect, or trust.

How do you receive input from a person you have written off as hateful? How do you deal with buts that derive from a rejected premise or that trigger some deep sense of loathing in you?

Jeff Goldblum has a penchant for playing characters who are the wrong messenger trying to deliver the right message. He does it in *Jurassic Park* as the relatively unlikeable Dr. Ian Malcolm. And in the movie *Independence Day*, his character struggles to deliver the warning of an alien attack to the U.S. President, because the two men have a history of animosity.

Unlike in *Jurassic Park*, however, Goldblum's character in *Independence Day* mends fences and transforms from the skeptic to the hero when he not only manages to identify the threat but works out a solution that delivers the movie's admittedly implausible deus ex machina. If the Two But Rule can turn Jeff Goldblum into a hero, imagine what it can do for you.

The inherent risk of applying the Two But Rule is starting with the 1But, which people accustomed to a positivity-first approach will find to be a turnoff. And if you've been negative in the past or if you've developed a reputation for being a skeptic, you have a messenger problem.

It may be cold comfort, but a long practice of applying the Two But Rule can help. Over time, consistently presenting solutions along with your concerns, your 2Buts with your 1Buts, will help colleagues become accustomed to expecting the positive punchline and giving you room to present all your buts.

The Empathetic But

Psychologist and conflict mediator Marshall Rosenberg grew up in Detroit and was influenced by living through the 1943 race riots that left 34 people dead and hundreds injured. He became interested in how people, who he believed were fundamentally compassionate, got to a place of anger and hatred toward each other. In his book *Nonviolent Communication, A Language for Life* he suggests that this arises from a failure to recognize and reflect our own needs and the needs of others. And one of the deepest, most pervasive needs we have as humans is simply the need to be heard.

By now we've established that the practice of Momentum Thinking starts with someone articulating their intent and then some form of "But that won't work," followed by "But it would work if...." But Rosenberg provides a helpful intermediate step, particularly when you aren't in a friendly, playful environment.

Before presenting your 1But, you can summarize and reflect not only what you heard the other person propose but how you understand it as an expression of their needs. For example, you might say, "I hear that you're suggesting we organize a community cleanup event. Am I right in thinking that you're excited about this because of your commitment to community engagement and environmental well-being?" Then, when you introduce your 1But, there's a better chance of receptivity. It can also prompt you to articulate your needs and how your issue with their idea expresses those needs.

Rosenberg's methods, like the Two But Rule, are both simple and nuanced. They deserve a full reading on their own, but it's easy to see how they're consistent with the point of Momentum Thinking: we honor the intentions of the other person, we honor our own objections, and we seek to square them in a way that meets everyone's needs.

When your intentions are in the right place, you can overcome interpersonal challenges and achieve momentum. And being in touch with both your needs and the needs of the person voicing issues with your idea will help you find solutions together.

Get this right, and you can dispense with tired techniques like the "positivity sandwich" for massaging feelings while delivering bad news or expressing concerns. People instinctively know that the praise you deliver before and after the negative feedback is usually as stale and soggy as two slices of Wonder Bread that have been left out in the rain. But if both sender and receiver of the feedback know to expect a 2But after the 1But, you can cut to the chase and build a more authentic relationship.

The But of an Ass

There are times when the intentions of the person presenting an idea or an obstacle may not be benign. Or you may simply not like the person. Or you just have other things to do.

If you want to maintain momentum while also not giving in to what your lucid and discerning mind has labeled "bullshit," there are ways to do it. Here are a few:

- "This isn't a conversation I want to have right now...BUT we could find a time later, and we should consider xyz in the meantime."

- "I think you have ulterior motives that are coloring what you just said, and I don't believe you are sincere in your exploration of the truth...BUT if you can show good faith, I can remain open."

- "Even though I believe your intentions are sincere, I don't like working with you, BUT I know someone else who can help."

If you get the sense that the person proposing something you object to has bad motives, swim away and reserve your buts for people focusing on solving real problems you care about. And remember—there's nothing in the Two But Rule that says you have to accept input from the but of an ass.

9

Old Buts and New Buts

One of the things that divides us and makes it hard to achieve Momentum Thinking together is an inability to hear each other across generational divides.

Take startup accelerators like Y Combinator, for example. Today, there are roughly 7,000 accelerators worldwide. They're run by investors, governments, and large corporations. Most emphasize their ability to make connections to talent, investors, services, and experienced mentors.

Connecting new startup founders with experienced executives, engineers, and scientists often means navigating the "we-tried-it-before" problem. We'll call it the *old but problem*.

Here's an example of how the old but problem usually plays out: A young and ambitious team says, "We're going to disrupt the hotel industry." Their slightly-long-in-the-tooth advisors say, "That's adorable, but we tried that in the 80s, the 90s, and 20 times since 2000, and it hasn't ever worked." Then the startup team, writing off the advisors as wrinkly, old 1But guys, gives it a shot anyway.

Airbnb and Paul Graham's Old But Breakthrough

Airbnb started life in 2007 but stumbled through various false starts until entering Silicon Valley startup accelerator Y Combinator in 2009. There they met experienced startup mentor Paul Graham, who helped spot a pattern in their rental listings. The listings that were getting booked had great photos, and the ones that weren't getting booked had photos that sucked. This made sense, but how could they improve the photos?

Graham gave them a brilliantly dumb idea, one that couldn't possibly scale. He told the founder team to buy some cameras and go take better photos for the customers. Result? Revenues doubled. Airbnb founder Joe Gebbia credits this moment as the company's turning point.

What Graham provided was a good example of Momentum Thinking: "But people aren't responding to your listings, because the photos suck. BUT they wouldn't suck if you personally shot better photos for the customers." From there, the team just had to follow the pattern: "But we can't scale making photos not suck that way, BUT we could if…."

Here's the thing. The old buts are often right. They ran the experiment. They possess the necessary data and detail from intimate firsthand experience about where, how, and why a set of lofty intentions came crashing down—not just once but multiple times.

In fact, Y Combinator execs today recall that they had heard the "let anyone rent their own apartment" pitch many times before. The typical reaction to the idea was that it had been done to death.

And yet, if the founders of Airbnb had decided not to try again or if they hadn't listened to Paul Graham's old but, millions of travelers today would still be forced to stay at a Motel 6, and the media would now be deprived of an endless series of click-bait horror stories of trashed apartments and homes turned into brothels.

The correct Two But Rule approach is obvious: "But we tried it before, and it didn't work, because...BUT you should try it again and watch out for the potholes and speed bumps we ran into." That's effectively what Paul Graham did. And instead of just pointing out what didn't work, he dug in and found workable problems, like bad photos. Instead of saying, "See, this is why this doesn't work," he applied Momentum Thinking and made his advice hard for the team to ignore.

Too often, the unnecessary tragedy is that the new but-heads completely ignore the old but-heads. Sure, in the age of big venture capital some projects can run over every pothole, hit every speed bump, and even crash through a few jersey barriers, and still make it across the finish line into the unicorn club. Even so, this is tragic, because clearly these unicorns have the resources to do better.

Today, more than a few of these companies have spent billions merely papering over the fundamental problems that they were meant to solve—sometimes without ever making a profit. Their investors, certainly the ones who funded later rounds, are still waiting to see a return. As George Santayana wrote in 1905, "Those who cannot remember the past are condemned to repeat it." (Yeah, Churchill said roughly the same thing.)

New but-heads should take advantage of the old but-heads, even if they don't need them. And the old farts should remember that the job isn't to prevent the newbies from making mistakes, including old mistakes. The job is to make sure that even if they're destined to run over that pothole that took out your rear axle 20 years ago, you can at least help them see it coming. You never know. They may have invented a better axle.

Runaway Buts

The Two But Rule is about not letting blockers or inertia bleed away the mental agility needed to succeed. But strangely, momentum itself can generate its own inertia. We tend to resist change and then suddenly lurch headlong into the new, new thing without question. We've somehow developed a culture that tends, once it embraces a trend, to silence dissent and succumb to groupthink. You have to wonder how long the engineers who saved the crew of Apollo 13, who demonstrated the ultimate form of optimism in their ability to nimbly embrace skepticism, would last in a typical organization today.

In his visually stunning book on creativity *Orbiting the Giant Hairball*, Gordon MacKenzie suggests that organizations become a kind of gravity well as they accumulate people. A new person entering the well with a very shallow orbit crashes into the "hairball," adding to its inertia. A person with a very eccentric orbit shoots past the hairball and is lost in space, while some people find a balanced, elliptical orbit. They're able to influence the hairball but not crash into it. Sometimes they're farther away, exploring. Sometimes they're closer in, returning what they found and influencing the tides.

The problem comes when the hairball takes on such overwhelming momentum in one direction that the orbiters can no longer alter its trajectory. Here's how this happens. First there's a status quo, filled with dogma, with everyone getting along. And then come the innovators, who sometimes succeed in changing things. Then a new status quo is achieved. New dogma. New inertia. This is fine, but there's a moment in this process that's particularly troublesome for exercising the Two But Rule.

At the top of the hype cycle of a new movement, the direction becomes even harder to change than the old status quo. Having worked so hard to change the old regime, the new regime has no interest in changing itself. The change they sought is too fragile. This makes them very sensitive to new, new ideas.

At moments like this, being in touch with intentions is especially important. Is your focus on improving the new effort, or is the motive to change the game that's already in the middle of changing someone else's game? If the latter, you're going to have a hard time.

The pull of a new direction can be so powerful that it can't allow any course corrections. No buts allowed. Pointing out any set of buts will fall on deaf ears. People will tend only to hear the 1But. They're moving too fast. The doppler shift of their runaway-train-thinking intensifies your 1But to a pitch that hurts their ears, and as they pass you by, it turns your 2But into an unintelligible drone of nonsense, fading out as they barrel along.

During this stage, the response you tend to get from the mavens of the new movement is, "I hear your concerns, but I don't agree with you." This is a classic 1But answer. It's the positivity police's very own 1But momentum killer.

This is why the Two But Rule is so important. It's the antidote to the dual scourges of toxic positivity and obstinate negativity. Perhaps, if more new movements arose from being 2Butted, rather than being ignored or 1Butted to death, they would be less resistant to new thinking during the formative years of their new order.

Without this, new movements tend to repeat the mistakes of the order they replace. And they do this often having invented much more powerful and efficient tools. They dote on their new tools, worshipping them as a way to transcend the evils of the old ways. But they forget to replace the component that seems supremely good at repeating history: the humans. Humans who now have better tools to amplify the old patterns. History is replete with this cycle: bone to bronze, bronze to iron, iron to steel. This all leads to an eerily familiar distribution of convenience and destruction.

In 1996, John Perry Barlow penned the defining work of the Internet era. It became a manifesto of the technical wizards and wild-eyed revolutionaries building the modern Web. He called it "A Declaration of the Independence of Cyberspace." Here's an excerpt:

> *"Governments of the Industrial World, you weary giants of flesh and steel, I come from Cyberspace, the new home of Mind. On behalf of the future, I ask you of the past to leave us alone. You are not welcome among us. You have no sovereignty where we gather."*

Barlow's generation built a massive network infrastructure, the World Wide Web, and they worshipped it as the god that would deliver them from the tyranny of governments and corporate corruption.

Today, many worship at the new alter of technology movements like "Web3," heaping scorn on priests of the old guard like Mr. Barlow. The Web3 evangelists are correct in pointing out that instead of transcending tyranny or ending the era of corporations, the World Wide Web became a favorite tool of those seeking to exert control over everyday people.

The current generation's solution? Decentralization. Blockchain. The dream of an unstoppable infrastructure controlled only by the people who use it, run by technical and human consensus. Sound familiar? Many of the proclamations of Web3 evangelists could have been written by Barlow himself.

It's not all fresh faces in the new order. The rebel leaders of the past, now firmly in power, pick the winners of the future. They remember being tut-tutted and ignored, ridiculed, and scorned for their previous ideas. They point triumphantly to the ultimate dominance of their past inventions. And now they proclaim their new favorites as inevitable winners.

More than a few heroic inventors of the Web—some now super-rich venture capitalists—are Web3's biggest supporters and financiers. One of their arguments for why Web3 is here to stay: the detractors of their previous stuff were wrong, so the naysayers must be wrong now.

Consider the problem with this argument. There are many forgotten technology movements that were once held up as the next big thing but have since fallen into obscurity. Their proponents, pushing back against the many buts that were shoved in their faces at the time, righteously said that they would prevail, because "nobody believed in the telephone, the Internet, or Beanie Babies before they became popular either." They were wrong…at least for now. (One never knows when a forgotten old idea will rise again.)

Just as we only remember successful startups, we conveniently forget about the dead branches of history. This makes it easy for even the smartest people to succumb to the "My thing is here to stay *because Internet*" fallacy.

The shame is that even if the new order is right about their new thing being here to stay, it will be more prone to repeating history, circling the drain toward a future that would seem both familiar and dystopian to their predecessors.

In this phase of mass groupthink, the "I have faith it'll work out" answer becomes the dominant reaction to all buts, killing momentum once again.

So, in addition to the momentum-killers of the positivity police and 1But-guy, beware of charging bulls. They have momentum, but some of them have trouble changing direction.

The End of Buts

History is riddled with failed projects. A poll by venture legend Bill Gross of IdeaLab suggests that the lion's share of startup failures are a result of bad timing. But really, if you look at specific cases, it's easy to argue that mainly they run out of buts. They get tired, which is a factor in timing failures, to be sure. They stop making adjustments, pivoting, and persevering. They come to an odd-numbered but and stop cold, not bothering anymore to add the next even-numbered but. And that's it. Game over. The response to any 1But may simply be, "BUT I'm ready to let this go and move on." As Mark Manson said in *The Subtle Art of Not Giving a F*ck*, "The truth is, I thought I wanted something, but it turns out I didn't. End of story."

One thing that Momentum Thinking can deliver is a straighter, shorter path to the realization that we didn't really want to overcome a problem or capture a particular opportunity after all. If you can't muster the energy and focus to go four or five rounds with the Two But Rule on your budding intention, then you can save yourself the time and expense of driving down a path to nowhere and running out of gas along the way.

Even if you're willing to see something through, time can still catch up with you, and the bell might strike on an odd-numbered but. The crew of Apollo 13 might not have made it home. There comes a moment when you are out of options and unable or unwilling to pivot. BUT, even at the bitter end we have choices about how we face reality. As Victor Frankl said, "When we are no longer able to change a situation, we are challenged to change ourselves." So we always have the opportunity for one last important but: "BUT I learned something about myself."

10

Putting Your But to Work

There are only two endings to a well-run process of Momentum Thinking: a decision to stop, as we just saw in the previous chapter, or a decision to go. This is about the latter, turning Momentum Thinking into Momentum Doing.

The most critical moment in applying the Two But Rule is when you realize that your cavalcade of 1Buts and 2Buts have produced enough creative juice to take action. It's when everything crystallizes into a plan that's not just technically feasible but psychologically acceptable to the team. This is the moment anxiety turns into collective excitement.

You could decide to continue piling up buts endlessly until that magic moment, but time is the ultimate but. And while a hallmark of more creative teams is the willingness to wrestle longer with a complex issue, playtime must always come to an end. The ending of play is an essential part of what makes it meaningful. So it's good practice to give around an hour and a half at minimum (and usually no more than three hours) to playing the 2Buts game.

When that time is up, whatever you have is what you're going to act on, no matter what. Taking that seriously will shift your exploration naturally from a lot of lateral thinking early in the session to the discovery of more practical, actionable 2Buts as the end of the session approaches.

Your 2Buts are becoming actionable when they attract enough support to pursue—and when they're based on clear, verifiable facts or readily testable assertions that can be translated into feasible actions.

Once you've selected which but to test, it's time to design an experiment. A good experiment should last as little as a few hours, typically a day or two, and rarely more than a week. If the experiment requires longer than that, it's likely that there are two or more smaller experiments hiding inside. Choose the smallest one you can that will likely reveal the most about the problem.

The experiment can take the form of simple research, talking to knowledgeable people, acting out the steps of a process, or building what some call a minimally viable product—MVP for short.

Product and startup people will recognize this as part of an agile, iterative process that serial entrepreneur Steve Blank pioneered and startup guru Eric Ries crystallized in his landmark book *The Lean Startup*. But the approach is practical in pretty much any context, even an everyday intention like deciding which classes to attend or which job offer to take.

In simplest terms, the Lean Startup approach applies scientific principles to testing the assumptions behind a new venture. Take the ride-hailing service Cabulous, for example. In 2009, there were apps on the market that allowed a passenger to book a cab or limo, but Cabulous had an assumption that there was something special and important about people actually seeing the car's position on their smartphone in something that looked like a street map. This might seem obvious to anyone accustomed to using Uber or Lyft today, but in 2009 it was not obvious that anyone really cared about seeing live cars driving around a smartphone map.

So the team fashioned a completely fake iPhone app in a couple of days. The app showed fake taxis driving around on a mocked-up version of Google Maps. The team then walked up to people who seemed as though they were trying to catch a cab, saying, "Hey, check this out!" Then they showed their iPhone screen to the test subjects. If the person enthusiastically pulled out their own iPhone and attempted to add the app, the team noted the reaction…before telling the subject that it was fake and giving them a coupon to get a hot dog from a nearby street vendor. Likewise, if the subject indicated that they didn't have an iPhone or that they used some other way to get a cab (or if they simply seemed uninterested), that too was noted by the team. The results of this tiny MVP experiment gave the team confidence that focusing on showing live cars on the map was the right thing to prioritize as they built the real thing.

Leaning Into Your But

There's a danger in the Lean Startup approach that can snare the unwary. As we saw earlier, the correct scientific method doesn't attempt to prove assumptions but to disprove them. This is just as important in the Lean approach. But it's easy for entrepreneurs to seek the emotional comfort of observations that validate their intentions and show they are on the right path.

In the Cabulous case, the initial plan was to keep deployment costs low by loading the app on taxi drivers' personal smartphones. This assumed that drivers actually had such a device. So the team conducted an experiment by calling all the taxi dispatchers in San Francisco and telling them that any driver who presented a smartphone at a popular donut shop on a certain night would receive a free donut and coffee. More than 100 drivers showed up, and a quarter of them had iPhones. The team considered this a terrific figure to start with.

Here's the catch. During this experiment, the team was laser-focused on finding out that there were enough drivers with smartphones. They weren't using the experiment to find all the problems that might be lurking in that plan.

Acting on the positive news about the percentage of drivers with smartphones, Cabulous committed resources and rolled out their app in early 2010. There was just one problem. Even though there were known passengers using the app and known drivers running the app on their phones, nobody was seeing taxis on the map, and drivers weren't getting rides.

What happened? It turns out that in those days, many drivers had altered their iPhones in a process called *jailbreaking*, and this allowed them to run the Cabulous app while talking on the phone. This made it seem, at first, as though everything was working fine. Unfortunately, because of the limitations of cellular networks in those days, data wouldn't flow to and from the smartphone while the driver was on the phone…and taxi drivers are always on the phone. That was an expensive mistake that could have been avoided if the team had conducted their early experiments in a 2Buts manner.

The key to the "Lean Into Your But" approach is to use the time to seek out new buts, new reasons why the idea won't work, to boldly show issues no one has seen before. This is not about proving yourself right. Instead, it's about learning more about the problem or opportunity and evolving the solution accordingly. It's about maintaining momentum by embracing those buts, joyously weighing the ones that matter and finding new solutions.

Pro tip: Give awards to team members who find new buts during the MVP or other experimentation phase. And be sure to give yourself a pat on the back for the ones you find. Put up a shrine. Call it The Wall of Buts (or something irreverent and memorable), and challenge the team to fill it up during each experiment. Then return to it at the end of the experiment and add 2Buts to each of the new 1Buts. Then it's back to the playground to start the process over again.

Another pro tip: It's sometimes powerful to designate one or two team members as honorable but-heads. (Possibly dress it up with a different moniker of your choosing, like Skepticism Services Manager, Chief Curmudgeon, or Negativity Czar, depending on the particulars of your team's sense of humor.) No matter what you call the role, it's important to honor, respect, and elevate the job of pointing out problems, wondering about weaknesses, and theorizing about threats. This approach is especially helpful if you have natural skeptics or contrarians on the team. We want to turn our but-heads from outcasts into heroes, and this is a really good way to start that process.

Encourage the team to see the designated skeptic as a kind of sonar operator telling you that there's a mine just ahead. Later, after you avoid the mine, you're going to give that guy a medal for saving the crew. And you're going to get a medal, too, for reacting with: "But we don't have to run into that mine, if we…." Or possibly, "But we don't have to sink after hitting that mine, if we…." Or at least, "But we can save a few people from drowning after we hit that mine, if we…."

Five Buts

The Lean Startup involves a practice called the "Five Whys," a way to find the root causes of a problem. Here's an example: **Why** did the ship blow up? (Because we hit a mine.) **Why** did we hit a mine? (Because the sonar operator was distracted by their iPhone.) **Why** was the iPhone a distraction? (Because the first mate sent them an adorable cat video.) **Why** was the cat video adorable? (Because cats are using social media to take control of society by addicting everyone to adorableness.) **Why** are cats trying to control society? (Because cats are an evil multidimensional alien species bent on dominating the universe.) So, as should have been obvious from the start, the root cause of the ship exploding was that cats are evil.

You might be tempted to think that a 2Buts approach would replace the Five Whys with the Five Why-Nots. The Two But Rule is a little different. It's not about saying "Why not" or "But that won't work" five times. Instead, we repeat the process of adding 2Buts to 1Buts five times.

"But if we rely on the sonar operator to alert us to mines, they're likely to be distracted by evil adorable cat videos. BUT we could outlaw sending adorable cat videos. But if we outlaw sending cat videos, the sonar operator will be distracted by their bad mood, because they won't be getting their daily dose of adorableness. BUT we could invite the cats aboard the ship to provide plenty of adorableness. But then the evil cats would have a harder time making videos to take over the world. BUT now that the sonar operator isn't distracted, we can collect all the mines and make an adorable video of blowing up the cats with the mines. But then we'd be fresh out of adorable cats and back to our lack-of-adorableness problem. BUT that video would be so adorable (and violent) that it would go viral and finally achieve the multidimensional cats' mission of world domination. Win-win. (But getting blown up isn't great for the cats, BUT because they're multidimensional, they probably won't mind being blown up in this dimension. And to thank us for our help, they might open a portal to their dimension, bathing the ship in adorableness and ensuring our sonar operator is never distracted again.)

It should be clear that five rounds of the Two But Rule can take you places that "Five Whys" can't...as long as you don't like cats.

The Two But Retrospective

Now that you've collected a series of Buts during your experiment, it's time to regroup and review. Your Wall of Buts should be filled with 1Buts by now, and the job is to ensure that each one is matched with a 2But. Then, once you've done this, you repeat the experiment process by looking for the most actionable 2But that will likely provide the most learning. In the case of the evil adorable cats, the obvious test that would have the most impact is to try outlawing sending cat videos for a day or two and monitoring the sonar operator's mood. If it turns out they don't mind not watching adorable cat videos, problem solved, and none of the admittedly awesome remaining buts needs to be tested (unless you really love blowing up evil multidimensional cats).

The point of all this is to make sure we reduce the chance of missing issues until it's too late, which would slow us down or stop us from achieving our ultimate goals. But how do we know when we've made it to the finish line? How do we make sure we aren't taking actions that are leading us further away from the goal?

Of course, there is no finish line. The most straightforward way to make sure your buts aren't leading you astray is to regularly include "But will this plan distract us from where we're trying to go?" The 2But that follows might be simply "BUT we can drop this idea and try again with the goal more firmly in mind." Or your 2But might surprise you: "Yes, this is going to take us someplace we weren't intending, BUT that destination looks like a better place to go."

Those are the basics of going from Momentum Thinking to Momentum Doing. We're nearly ready to tackle a sea of big gnarly challenges. But first, there's one more thing. We're going to need all the heavy equipment we can get for handling whole truckloads of very big buts.

CHAPTER

11

Managing Your But

After walking through just a few short rounds of Momentum Thinking, you can see that it doesn't take much to find yourself up to your neck in buts. It's no wonder that we see so few cases of using the Two But Rule in the media, during meetings, or in the halls of government. There just isn't enough room, not enough time, and not enough patience. Even cases later in this book will have to leave a lot of buts on the cutting room floor to keep the page count short of the full *Game of Thrones* boxed-set edition.

Without help, our busy lives barely have time for an occasional game of 1But. It's understandable that society is developing an abhorrence to opposition. The no-buts policy might be an intellectual and innovative dead end, but it can be less annoying than a mob 1Butting each other to death.

That said, applying the Two But Rule can be fast, as we saw with Apollo 13. It can lead to fewer mistakes that would otherwise cost time and lead to disaster later, as we saw with Volkswagen. And there is a lot less friction involved in exploring issues when people know they can expect a second but after someone points out a problem with an idea.

Still, running five rounds of the 2 Buts game can be exhausting mentally, especially for a team. And if you need to discuss or write down all the "But that won't work, BUT it would if...But that also won't work, BUT it would ifs...," you're going to run out of room fast. We're going to need some help exercising our buts. We need a few tools and techniques.

2But Tools

The simplest thing needed to help build a habit of applying the Two But Rule is universal understanding. When you say, "Hey, I'd like to tell you some problems I see with your idea," you need your colleague to say, "Oh! Cool, let's do some Momentum Thinking on that." But, well...that's just super boring. There's a reason this book is called *The Two But Rule* and not *The Practice and Application of Momentum Thinking for Problem-Solving and Innovation*. It's more fun if your colleague says, "OK, then, show me your buts." At least it's harder to forget.

When it comes to applying the Two But Rule in meetings, there's a time factor. The same goes for journalism, reports, or anything with limited space. Ever notice that even the best on-camera interviewers let politicians get away with hardly a single pair of buts?

"But Senator, some say your proposal is too expensive."

"Yes, Barbara, they say that, but it's not too expensive."

"Oh! OK, then, next question."

In a 2 Buts world, we can learn to shift our buts in time and space. There is no reason every article can't come with a link to an expanded page full of buts. It's a trivial matter today to make such pages interactive. In fact, the comments section of any article can be rigged to prompt for two buts: "We really want to hear your thoughts, but extra points if you apply the Two But Rule."

In a 2Buts world, there might even be people standing by to help you handle your but. Getting ready to do a brainstorming session? An innovation or design workshop? A planning meeting? Make sure to upgrade it to one equipped with the Two But Rule.

Finally, you can shift a lot of buts into breakout sessions, as we saw with the drunken science interns case in Chapter 7. In fact, designating specific junior team members as official but handlers—on second thought, best to call it something else—can help ensure that breakout teams return with bags full of beautiful, well-organized buts.

Two But Notation

In many cases, it's sufficient to combine a 1But, its "because" statement, and a 2But in a single paragraph, moving to the next paragraph for the next set of buts. In the cases in Section 3, we'll write 1Buts normally (But) followed by 2Buts in all caps (BUT).

For more complex explorations, there are numerous tools now on the market that allow flowcharting or mind mapping. Even simple block-organizing tools like Obsidian or Notion that allow cross-linking can help get your buts in line, articulate a ton of insights, and keep track of them as you explore.

Artificial Buts

Even with all these tools and techniques, the practice of Momentum Thinking would be hobbled by the weight of all those buts—and the Two But Rule might be little more than an amusing coffee table book—had it not been for the explosion of practical artificial intelligence in 2023. Suddenly, we have a real Momentum Thinking machine.

When it comes to gnarly problems, the depth and breadth of branching involved in piling 2Buts upon 1Buts, not to mention endless side buts, starts to look like a Banyan tree that's been fed with radioactive Miracle Grow. It's going to tax anyone's stamina to read, let alone produce, a lot of buts this way. As I said earlier, this explains why we don't see more application of the Two But Rule in the media or any forum that has to comply with time limits and attention spans. That's where AI comes in.

AI is so important to managing and scaling the practice of applying the Two But Rule to real-world issues that it's worth a brief digression on AI's recent history and attributes.

Large language models, chat bots, machine learning, fancy statistics—whatever you call it, we're all talking about artificial intelligence these days…a lot.

Like the Internet in 1999, smartphones in 2007, and fidget spinners in 2017, AI is having its moment, and it's a big one. OpenAI's ChatGPT became the fastest growing consumer application in history in 2023, breaking 100 million daily active users in just two months. Since then, the number of new ChatGPT applications and users has grown so fast that it's hard to keep up.

But there are some interesting issues with this technology. Currently, popular AI chatbots can provide incorrect answers, and ChatGPT does so with such linguistic confidence that it's easy to believe it, even when it's obviously wrong. Beyond incorrect answers, LLMs can demonstrate "mindless discomprehension," a condition pundits have begun calling AI hallucinations. Beyond hallucinations, LLMs can produce biased responses as a result of ingesting biased training data, and efforts to prevent this have famously resulted in accusations of more bias.

(I asked ChatGPT about this, and it concurred. To paraphrase: "LLMs like me can generate biased responses and lack common sense. —Love, ChatGPT…XOXO.")

With hugely popular applications like ChatGPT and the generative-art app Dall-E, OpenAI indeed prioritized interesting answers over correct results. Is the image that Dall-E makes when you ask for a picture of Elon Musk riding Joe Rogan like a donkey on Mars accurate? Well, the one I just produced with a similar AI called Midjourney seems to have decided that Joe Rogan is just a donkey with a Darth Vader mask on. Not remotely accurate…but interesting? Yes…in a peyote fever-dream sort of way.

In any event, there's something to be said for using AI hallucinations as a feature, not a bug. But what does all this mean for Momentum Thinking? It means everything. AI doesn't know everything (yet), and like many humans, it tends to "misremember" and make things up, but it's definitely there to get you thinking.

Two-But Buddy

It's difficult, working on your own, to clearly see your but—let alone to embrace both sides of it. And getting someone else to help can be too intimate, and possibly inappropriate, even for the closest of colleagues. We've already seen the challenges of getting whole teams to expose their buts to each other.

But now you have a friend who can help, one who will never judge you for what might be hiding in your but. (At least I don't think so.) And it can really help with organizing, expanding upon, and exploring complex groups of 1Buts and 2Buts. Meet your new two-but buddy: ChatGPT (or, if you prefer, Google Bard, Microsoft Bing, or any of the many, many alternatives popping up every day).

When you're stumped or stuck searching for buts, particularly the all-important 2But, ChatGPT can be strangely helpful in getting into the flow and turbocharging the process. You can get started simply by asking ChatGPT to give you some issues it sees with what you want to do and then telling it to give you solutions to each of those issues. Then you can repeat the process. I do this all the time these days, multiple times a day. Here are a few tips on how to create 2But prompts:

> *"I intend to [intention to overcome a problem or capture an opportunity here]. Give me [#] reasons why this intention won't work. Use the form, "But that won't work, because...". Then for each of those issues, provide [#] of ways to solve the issue. Use the form, "But it could work if..."*

After ChatGPT provides a response, prompt with this:

> *"Provide [#] new issues for each of the previous solutions and [#] new solutions for each of the new issues."*

Variations include using the following phrases in your prompts: "out of the box," "step by step," "practical and actionable," "totally crazy." Yes, AI can now be "totally crazy" for you.

Chatbots are all the rage these days, but we can go further with future AI tools for Momentum Thinking. Imagine a browser plugin that took any story and created a user's own database of buts, highlighting particularly interesting and unexpected ideas and issues, 1Buts and 2Buts. Such a treasure chest filled with an accumulation of buts over years could become extraordinarily valuable.

Why not build a habit of ingesting everything we read—any email, message, article, book, or video transcript—directly into our own personal data vault? This might sound crazy, but it's happening right now. We could selectively share our buts and invite others to add more buts to our own. Our AIs could then elaborate things further by connecting new buts to relevant existing buts and creating new, unexpected buts based on the AI's growing insight into our interests and ways of thinking.

Apps and browser extensions that automate the capture and processing of our communication and browsing history are appearing in the marketplace. Email providers will be adding it as a service. You could have a 2But sidebar on any web page and in any meeting software. Arguments and assertions in a story can be automatically identified, with their buts presented in the sidebar.

Tools like these are important, because some really gnarly problems (like regulating AI) require the careful and comprehensive management of vast arrays of buts. Just in time. Government decision-makers are sorely in need of better but management. Rather than simply repeating political party talking points, endlessly arguing past each other, and being forced into lazy compromises, politicians could do better in some cases applying the Two But Rule. AI could be helpful here. Rather than waiting for political parties to embrace each other's buts, issues before them could be run through a 2But AI to generate whole arrays of buts that the members might never have stopped to think about.

Protecting Your Buts

A word of caution. The data about your buts must be protected, and you need to maintain sole control over it. Let it get copied to a system controlled by someone else, and you've handed them your but…forever.

So, be sure to use apps and services that explicitly grant you sole ownership of those AI conversations, and use only those that make it easy for you to control who sees them.

You might allow a platform to use your data in exchange for added value services such as searching for others with similar interests. However, the minute you share any of this kind of information to anyone, you have no way of knowing ultimately who will wind up looking at your but.

Teaching AI to Embrace Its But

I wrote this book for you and me, for people who have ideas and are looking for a way to make them real without making a mess in the process, and for people with vision who are too sensible to ignore the buts on the way to the goal.

Yet, this book might not ultimately be for any of us. In getting AI to help us manage our buts, we're teaching it to practice the art of the Two But Rule. The more 2Buts content on the Internet, the more 2Buts conversations we conduct with ChatGPT and other forms of AI, the more the *fancy math* going on in an AI system will find itself in a 2Buts habit. And that might be a very good thing. The day that Dr. Evil tells his AI sidekick to execute his nefarious plan to take over the world, it might happen to reply, "But that's a terrible plan, because what you really want is for your mommy to love you, and this will just make a lot of mommies hate you, BUT we could try this other plan instead."

Now that we know how to manage our buts, it's time to put them to work on real-life issues. Let's go!

3

Life's Big Buts

CHAPTER

12

You and Your But

Now that we know how to get our buts in shape, share them with others, and manage them at scale, we're ready to take on truly thorny challenges—to overcome the hardest, most complex problems and capture the most innovative and unexpected opportunities.

We're about to find out how well our new but muscles perform to tackle various challenges, from everyday personal hindrances to big career-related questions and the complexities of starting and running your own business. We'll also talk about untangling new products and technologies, resolving social and political conflict, and finally the small matter of saving the world from calamity.

Each of these cases will present one or more intentions and a series of buts arranged loosely in pairs...naturally.

An odd-numbered but will look like this: But.

An even-numbered but will look like this: BUT.

Easy peasy.

We'll start with a pretty simple case and get progressively more ambitious. You may, along the way, experience but fatigue. That's OK. I didn't say that Momentum Thinking was easy. This isn't a book about decluttering your life. I'm not Marie Kondo. If the world were straightforward and simple, we wouldn't need the Two But Rule.

That said, for every pair of buts in the following cases, you're likely to see opportunities to add your own buts, such as in places where you see other options not explored or where the case doesn't go deep enough. Good! That's the point. Write those down, and start adding your buts to the story.

With that said, hold onto your buts. Here we go.

Everyday Buts

There are any number of stories about applying the Two But Rule to running companies, building products, and finding break-throughs, but it's important first to remember that it's a useful tool for our everyday lives.

Just because a problem or opportunity is subject to the confines of our personal lives doesn't mean it can't be frustratingly complex. In the grand scheme of starting businesses, managing global conflict, and saving ourselves from calamities like plastic pollution and climate change, a poopy diaper might not seem like a big problem. But tell that to a single parent in the middle of delivering a career-making speech on a livestream with 100 people watching, especially when there's no help in the house, the baby is screaming, and it's one of those diaper-destroying blow-out poops that shoot up the child's back and into their hair.

The poopy diaper problem may actually have no workable solutions under the current laws of physics, but here are a couple challenges from my personal experience. Let's start with a simple one that didn't feel so simple at the time.

Fixing the Fan

My youngest child recently grew tall enough to stand on their bed's footboard and pull on the chain that controls the ceiling fan. So, of course, they promptly broke it. The chain was made of those little metal beads connected to each other by little metal threads. The chain broke, and the end that was connected to the on-off switch was now hidden inside the fan's metal housing.

My Intention: Fix the fan. Earn points with my spouse. Possibly get lucky.

But, I couldn't get to the tag end of the chain stuck inside the housing to reconnect it. BUT I could if I managed to take off the housing and access the inside. After fumbling around trying to figure out how to do that, I managed to get the housing off. I'm happy to say that I did this without pulling the fan clean out of the ceiling when I fell off the chair that I was using as a stepladder.

But even with the housing off, the part of the chain still connected to the fan was too short to push through the housing, which I had to do in order to connect it to the rest of the chain that had broken off. BUT I figured that I could reverse the problem and push the broken-off part of the chain through from the outside of the housing and reconnect it.

But because of the way the chain was made, it was wobbly and I couldn't get it to go through the weirdly long tunnel in the housing simply by pushing it. Why was there a *tunnel* in the housing and not just a simple hole that I could have easily pushed the damn chain through? That's a mystery well outside the scope of this book to address. BUT in a flash of 2Buts insight, I scurried off to the kitchen, found a toothpick, and connected it to the chain with some tape. Then I pushed the rigid toothpick through the tunnel, grabbed it on the other side, and pulled the chain through. From there, it was a simple matter of using the little metal connector bracket that comes with these kinds of chains to connect the broken segments and reattach the housing. *Voilà!* I fixed the fan in just six buts.

But, now my shoulders were on fire, and I'd tweaked my back by holding my arms above my head for 20 minutes. BUT I had Advil. So…eight buts. (Getting credit with my spouse for my heroic act, and cashing in on those credits, involved more buts.)

Sure, you might not need to read a whole book on Momentum Thinking to fix a fan, and it's anyone's guess whether I'd have stumbled on the toothpick solution if I hadn't been actively contemplating the Two But Rule at the time. But let's look at a slightly more gnarly personal problem.

Surviving Parenting Purgatory

I have to take my 10-year-old to gymnastics practice three nights a week, for three hours each night. There's nobody nearby to carpool with, and there's nothing to do there but sit in a crappy metal chair and contemplate oblivion.

My Intention: Make better use of the time in gymnastics parent purgatory.

But it's hard to get anything useful done there, because it's the end of the day, I'm tired, and it's easy to wind up just talking to the other suffering parents until it's over. BUT I could bring noise canceling headphones and put on some soothing music to get into the zone for productive work on my laptop.

But so far that hasn't worked, because I start talking to the parents before I put the headphones on, BUT I could put them on before I go in.

But so far that hasn't become a habit, because again, I'm tired and not really in the mood at that moment to get into more work after a whole day of work. BUT maybe it's safe to drop my kid off and go home.

But it's 30 minutes to get there from my house, which is a lot of gas and time wasted to go there and back twice each night. BUT I could go hang out at a local Starbucks.

But now that just breathing the air in a Starbucks will set me back $10, it could get expensive going there three times a week. BUT I could go there and not order anything most of the time.

But I'm not comfortable with sitting for hours three times a week at a Starbucks without buying something. BUT I could start driving for Uber and take a few rides after I drop the kid off until I've made enough to offset the cost of a grande latte.

But I'm pretty sure I'd blow through my productivity time picking up enough Uber rides to pay for Starbucks. BUT there are other free "third places" that I could go, including the houses of friends who live near the gym.

I should say that I live in a large metro area made up of several cities connected by one congested highway. I see friends living in those other cities less often than friends living on the other side of the country, which feels awful. It happens that the gym is located at the midpoint of that highway. So at least on some nights I could go the extra distance and have a drink with friends. (Action that!)

But I still need a quiet place for most nights, and I notice that a key part of the problem is my brain fatigue at that time of day. BUT then why not join a gym nearby? I can look into that, and I need to get in better shape anyway. (Action that!)

But if I'm honest, I still feel better about staying at gymnastics most nights, because I'm a shameless helicopter parent. BUT I could propose to my kid's gym owners some kind of fitness program for the parents. (Crazy but?) OR! I could get the new Apple Vision Pros—the cool virtual reality headsets that cost a whopping $3,500 and look like a pair of ski googles. I could put them on before going into the gym. That would give me my virtual quiet place and allow me to block out all distractions. I'm definitely the sort of tech nerd that would shamelessly walk into a public place with a contraption on my head. Truth—I was looking for an excuse to get these anyway, and if they save me going to Starbucks 350 times, they'll pay for themselves! (Action that!)

But the chairs at the gym still suck, BUT I could bring my own comfy chair with me.

But a comfy chair usually means a bulky chair that I couldn't easily lug with me. BUT maybe I can find an amazing portable chair at REI or someplace. (Action that!) OR maybe I can get the gym to create a special area with theater seating for parents who are willing to pay extra. It's worth asking.

So, those sound like a few good options, and it gives me an argument I've been looking for to convince my wife she should let me buy a freakishly expensive Apple product. That's a win.

To sum it up, Momentum Thinking provided several solutions, several actions, and a few crazy new business ideas in 22 buts. Not bad!

Having looked at a couple of smaller (but still obviously thorny) life problems, let's consider one of life's biggest personal challenges.

Changing Careers

There are few situations that paint a clearer picture of the need for the Two But Rule than the challenge of course-correcting your life.

Have you ever wanted to change careers? Even if you're reasonably content doing what you're doing, take a second and consider whether you have a dormant desire to do something different. Start adding up the buts. But…But…But….

There are so many gaps between where you are now and where you want to go. Are you seeing all the missing qualifications, connections, and know-how to succeed in something new?

If you're like me, you're feeling a significant amount of discomfort looking at all those *impossibilities*. Here's the thing. Most of the time, you aren't wrong about the challenges ahead. And all the optimism, all the anecdotal success stories, all the willpower in the world will not change certain realities. This is a factor for everyone, young and old alike. We're going to look at several career changes here. But if my experience is any guide, buts get bigger as we age. So let's first consider the late-career change.

Let's say you're responsible for providing for a family and want to end your career as a corporate executive to pursue acting. You don't get to say, "I'm going to move the family from Des Moines to Los Angeles and start auditioning for movies, and I'll succeed if I just believe in myself enough." No. Sorry. There's a better way.

Start by listing everything that's non-negotiable. Everything you won't give up. Don't say you *can't* give it up. You *can* decide to sell the house and have your family live out of a station wagon while you go on auditions. But you won't. At least—I'm with your spouse on this one—I hope you won't.

Starting with your list of non-negotiables is strangely liberating. It disabuses you of magical thinking that keeps buzzing around your change fantasy. The problem is that most people stop there. For those unacquainted with the Two But Rule, this list is scary. It's the end of the line: "I want to change careers, but I won't give up the loss in salary that would certainly come from me starting over at the bottom with no experience, connections, or reputation." That's a big momentum killer.

So what do some career gurus tell you to do instead? "Think positively. Believe in yourself." That's "cruel and unusual" advice, really. It's a guaranteed headache. It solves nothing, and the lapses in judgment you'll make in pursuing your dream with a positivity blindfold on could easily land you in that station wagon…likely alone, because your spouse is going to take the kids and go live with their mother.

Most people won't take action and pursue their intentions if they look at the obstacles, but remaining willfully blind to them is a good way to fail. Worse, the latter is a path to quiet desperation as your dreams take flight while your unexamined, subconscious awareness of unacceptable trade-offs keeps you miserably rooted in place.

BUT this isn't a problem when you know how to apply the Two But Rule. You know that the non-negotiables are just grist for the mill—the start, not the end. You're going to take all those big 1Buts and relentlessly find 2Buts, even crazy ones.

Here's one you can try on your spouse: "I want to give up my six-figure job and become an actor, but the non-negotiables are that you won't give up being a stay-at-home parent, we won't give up our house, and we won't stop contributing to the kids' college fund," BUT is one of your non-negotiables that you won't change your approach to living? What if there are other families in the community facing career changes? Would you consider multifamily home living? It's a choice that was featured in the documentary *Happy* about a 20-family community in Denmark that cooks for each other and jointly takes care of the kids. Is there a story in your future about forming the "Actors' Enclave," a co-op community in Los Angeles made up of former corporate executives who banded together to raise families and support each other as they pursued their dreams of breaking into the movies? Maybe not, but who knows where this line of thinking might lead you.

Everyone's story is different. Consider the case of actor and comedian Ken Jeong. Ken was a practicing physician for more than a decade. He wasn't willing to give that up, so he started performing standup on the side, first in North Carolina while studying at Duke and then in New Orleans during his residency. But, breaking into the comedy big leagues was going to be tough while working as a physician in Louisiana, BUT doctors are in demand everywhere. So, he moved to Los Angeles and joined Kaiser Permanente as an internist. Then he got married. Later, Ken decided to quit his job and become a full-time comic actor, but his wife was newly pregnant…with twins. Quitting a job at that moment might have been a reckless move, BUT Ken had continued performing standup in Los Angeles before the kids were born and landed a few television roles. He got his big break when he was cast as Dr. Kuni in Judd Apatow's *Knocked Up*. The rest is history.

Ken had become a successful actor and comedian, but he didn't want to give up being a doctor. BUT he managed to maintain his status as a licensed physician. He frequently uses that experience in his comedy. And who knows? Maybe he has a lucrative side hustle treating fellow actors on set and writing marijuana prescriptions when shooting in states that only permit medicinal use.

Here's another case. We've explored how intentions matter. Intentions and understanding what's behind them. Say you have a good job in the brewing industry, and you happen to be very tall. You've decided to chuck it all for your love of horse racing. Instead of ignoring the impediments to becoming the world's first 58-year-old, 6-foot-7 jockey, you can start by observing what your true intentions might be. What's driving you from your cushy job as a beer tester to the world of equine racing?

This is a good moment to fuzz up the objective. What do you love about the idea of being a jockey? Is it that you like to be on tall, dangerous things that go fast? Is it the intoxicating smell of dirt and manure? If you just love being at the track, maybe shift from beer tasting to beer sales rep and angle yourself into the territory that sells to racetracks. Whatever it is, you can get underneath the real drivers of your intent a lot easier if you don't say "I want to be a horse jockey" and then recoil in shame and disappointment as you realize that you're too tall. Embrace that but.

The most common impediment to career course correction for both the old and the young is not knowing what you want to do and what you'd be good at.

I employed an intern a few summers ago during the pandemic. This person was brilliant. Energetic. Ambitious. And like so many interns, they were driven by a fire to make a difference in this world.

A few months after the internship was over, they called to say, "I've decided I want to dedicate my career to...," and then they proceeded to describe the technology we had been working on during the internship." My reply: "So you want to sell hammers."

I could tell they were puzzled, so I explained that whether it was relational databases, object-oriented programming languages, middleware, machine learning APIs, or blockchains, I'd spent half my career making and pushing *hammers*. Tools.

I like hammers. Someone has to invent, design, manufacture, and sell them. And as my old boss used to say, "You can put your kid through college by selling a good hammer." It turns out some of us can make a living just exploring what a hammer can and can't do.

I didn't think this intern was a hammer person. They were, thankfully, a "fix the world" person. It needs a lot of fixing.

Hammer-thinking can be a real trap for someone like that: "I want to solve world hunger...with this shiny hammer." That's the trap. It takes your eyes off the hunger problem and the people suffering from it.

There's an old exercise that designers use to make this point. They'll ask you to design a flower vase and give you a minute to sketch your ideas, which usually come out as one would expect... vase-like. And then they'll ask you to design a way for blind people—or people with some other specific quality—to enjoy cut flowers in the home. Totally different picture.

The point here is pretty simple: if you want to be sure you get to the end of your life confident you contributed more than you consumed, don't focus on the tool. Not a hammer, a nail…not even a house you can build with them. Focus on specific people who need shelter. Then, assemble all the tools you can find and use the ones that make sense.

That's what I recommend to most people these days when they ask me about dedicating their career to something. As an investor in one of my companies once said, "We don't fund people in love with their solution to a problem. We fund people who have an authentic story about why they will stop at nothing to solve a problem worth solving, even when their first, second, and third ideas don't work."

It's easy to say that one should focus on people and get to work helping them solve their problems. But once you open your mind—even a little bit—to a world full of people with problems, you're instantly overloaded. Too…many…people. Too…many…problems.

Suddenly you're that person on a crowded street, hearing calls for help from everywhere. Surely more qualified people to help are nearby. Where are the police? Where's the fire department?

It's easy to get overwhelmed by a sea of troubles. And it's especially hard for people like that intern—a middle-class kid from the United States for whom the clear and present dangers of the world aren't as "present" as they are for some—to choose one thing to tackle.

BUT it can help to methodically "pay attention to what you pay attention to." What do you notice even when nobody is pointing it out? What do you find yourself looking up on Google or ChatGPT when nobody is prompting you to research something?

But if you're like me, this doesn't work on the first try. Because when I—a hammers person—do this, I find myself looking up…yep, hammers. BUT luckily I've learned to let my mind wander a bit. I've developed the habit of consistently sitting for exactly 1.5 hours at a time doing absolutely nothing. The first half-hour in my head is usually all hammers. But then…magic. Do this for a week or three and then take account of whether you notice a consistent theme.

Another trap is thinking that you aren't qualified to play a role. Sometimes you may not be in a situation that gives you an advantage for solving a particular problem. BUT you are never disqualified. Sure, it's wise to keep looking for things that both attract your attention and for which you show some aptitude. But it's not necessary to be an expert in advance of diving in.

After years working on trying to make life suck less for taxi drivers, I could probably write a PhD thesis on the topic of ground transit. But when I decided to start a business on that topic, I knew next to nothing. BUT I wound up reading a ton and spending nights and days riding shotgun with taxi drivers and doing the night shift in dispatch centers. I learned fast.

If you're just starting out, you can dive into internships and work for all kinds of organizations, from startups to nonprofits. Keep iterating. You'll find your thing. And if you are already working hard to maintain the status quo, then you need to get clever, like Ken Jeong did. You might not be a doctor who can work anywhere, but it's certainly true that your life contains the makings of what you need to pivot into the life you truly intend to pursue.

If, after choosing what you aim to do, your main 1But is that you need more time than you have to learn new skills and build a network, here are some thoughts from Paul Graham. (It turns out he has good ideas for all of us, not just Silicon Valley unicorn founders.)

Graham says, "The way to figure out what to work on is by working. If you're not sure what to work on, guess. But pick something and get going. You'll probably guess wrong some of the time, but that's fine. It's good to know about multiple things; some of the biggest discoveries come from noticing connections between different fields." That, by the way, includes whatever your current field is. And that's the clue to your first 2But: BUT there is very likely a connection between what you're doing now and what you want to do that gives you not only a unique point of view but a way to start making baby steps in the new direction.

These days, there a lot more ways to take those baby steps than ever before. AI tools are making it very inexpensive to build businesses of your own, especially if the project involves deploying a new web or mobile application. Ideas that required hiring an engineering team to start a project just a few years ago can be developed and deployed with little to no help and some spare time. And even without the magic of ChatGPT, other platforms such as YouTube, Udemy, and Coursera contain step-by-step tutorials that will teach you just about anything.

It's clear that momentum is essential for getting out of the old and into the new. And now you have the tools to manage it. When you say to yourself, "But I don't know what's next for me," you know how to add, "BUT I would know if...."

Finding a good 2But in a moment of big changes is like being Neo from *The Matrix*, receiving a cookie from the Oracle. Your problem may not be solved yet, but you are starting to feel better already...*I guarantee it*.

13

Business Buts

The next three cases involve different types of businesses, including a small local coffee shop that shows how small businesses deal with big challenges, a high-tech startup that leap-frogged over every but standing in its way, and companies dealing with team dysfunction and the challenges of deciding whether to return to the office after the pandemic or commit to managing a remote-work organization for good.

Running a Small Business Is a Pain in the But

Small businesses are a big deal for the neighborhoods they serve, especially the ones that create and maintain the "third places" that form the backbone of a community's sense of belonging, its common ground. Speaking of common grounds, there's no more iconic example of this kind of essential small business than the local independent coffee shop.

In 2004, Raleigh sculptor David Benson, at the age of 54, decided to change careers and buy a local coffee shop. Conveniently for this story, it's called The Third Place. One of the first independent coffee shops in Raleigh, it occupies a spit of land that juts into an oddly shaped five-way intersection north of the city called Five Points. Dave quickly learned a lot about everyday buts running this place.

I should mention that The Third Place is *my third place* when I need to get away from the house or the office. They have decent Wi-Fi, and the coffee is high-octane.

Sitting with me on a hot summer afternoon, Dave gave me a full rundown of the many big and little buts that make up the flow of his life as a small business owner.

He spoke about times when a new drink or food item suddenly became popular. Customers started demanding it, but he had no space for it in the case or behind the counter. BUT, with a little creative shuffling, he usually found a way to make it work.

He described a popular sandwich that was a big seller, but it was too hard to make and wasn't very profitable, given all the ingredients, BUT they managed to turn it into a weekly special.

As the shop grew, Dave wanted to add more revenue-generating items, but he couldn't afford to add overhead. BUT, in keeping with the mission of The Third Place to serve the community, he displayed pieces by local artists and craftspeople all over the walls and counters and sold them on consignment. They made money. He made money. And it added to the unique ambiance of the cozy interior.

Everything was going well. And then the pandemic hit in 2020. Dave remembers hearing the news and shutting everything down a day later. He lost all but a few of his staff. Dave was about to lose his business as the neighborhood lost all its *third places*.

The remaining team tried to find a way to stay afloat, but, like most local independent coffee shops, they lived on razor-thin margins at the best of times. They didn't have much time to act, and they were out of options. BUT then Dave's partner, JJ Johnston, remembered her time as a call-center operator and proposed opening up a hotline for people to call in their orders and pick them up at the window.

The to-go option turned out to be a big hit. A similar strategy became a lifeline for many food businesses across the country in the early days of the pandemic. But Dave's team was quickly overwhelmed by the order flow, and their antiquated phone system couldn't handle the load. They were losing business and soon would have lost the interest of customers fed up with waiting on hold to order a coffee and a pastry. BUT then a loyal customer heard about the problem and donated the needed call-center equipment. They were back in business.

As the pandemic wore on and isolation restrictions were reduced, The Third Place's small team had to prepare for opening its doors again. They needed capital to add staff and make significant changes to the interior, including barriers and booths to isolate tables from each other. Dave tried to access the U.S. government's business relief funding program, but he found the banking system overwhelmed with requests. He was getting nowhere. BUT then another loyal customer with connections at a nearby bank gave Dave the name of someone there who could help with the paperwork and shepherd him through the process. The Third Place had the money it needed three days later. (Support from the community is the ultimate 2But for a small business.)

Dave remembers many other buts along the way to recovery. After they reopened, which increased their costs, many people weren't ready to come back inside. So they tried adding a pastry counter outside. That didn't work. They tried putting pictures of the items on the windows. Still no joy. BUT they discovered that staples like bags of granola had become big sellers. They were easy to list on window signs and could be located close to the entrance.

Even with these changes, returning to normalcy wasn't a smooth transition. Public isolation restrictions were lifted one day only to be reinstated the next. This made it hard to schedule staff and keep customers. When things finally returned to normal and customers could rely on The Third Place maintaining regular hours, Dave discovered a new issue he wasn't expecting. He couldn't find enough staff willing to return to work to fill the hours. That was a big but.

BUT through the pandemic years, Dave's little team became a tight operation, and they learned some things about the ebb and flow of business from to-go orders. This gave them the idea of limiting hours to coincide with high-order times. They tried a few different schedules. Longer hours on some days, shorter on others. But the lack of daily consistency led to confusion and threatened to lose customers. BUT they finally decided to open every day from 7am to noon. That solved the consistency problem, and that's how The Third Place operates today.

But, as I pointed out to Dave during our conversation, the neighborhood is now missing a *third place* to go after noon. No third place to get some writing or thinking in after midday. No third place to get together in the early evenings with friends. Dave receives frequent requests from people in the neighborhood to extend their hours. So far, it's just not in the cards or the economics.

At the end of our conversation I presented Dave with an idea of my own: "We all want you to stay open longer. But you still can't cover the staff, and you have the data to show that staying open after noon isn't profitable. BUT you could turn The Third Place into a community co-op, kind of like retailer REI. Members could earn a key card to get access at any time of day, the way some 24-hour fitness centers do it. An honor system, backed up by cameras and records of who entered and exited, would reduce the potential for damage or theft. The community investment would help with overhead, and member-customers could earn dividends, redeemed in coffee and food."

I was very proud of my clever idea, but Dave just smiled and pointed out the biggest 1But of all for a small business owner (really any sized business). He said, "I love that idea, but I'm doing everything I can just to keep the lights on. It's not on my list of things I can even make the time to research."

OK, it's hard to argue with Dave's logic, but…BUT maybe if I were to write a 2Buts case about The Third Place, it might become the preferred coffee shop for but-heads everywhere, a tourist destination attracting people from all over the world seeking good coffee and a chance to trade 2But stories. And then, maybe, Dave will consider my idea. It's worth a shot.

Calendly and the Many Buts of Starting a Business

I began this book by identifying a few gnarly problems you might be struggling with. One you might remember was "You're starting a company, but you're broke," suggesting that you might find answers to that problem here. It's time to pay off that promise.

Tope Awotona thought he had a new idea. He was so sure about it that he burned through his personal savings, took out a loan, and liquidated his retirement account to pursue it. By his own account, he made every kind of mistake starting this business. And yet, as you'll see, he never let a but slow his momentum on the way to making Calendly a break-out success.

Tope studied business information systems at the University of Georgia and came from a family of Nigerian entrepreneurs. He was working as an enterprise software salesman in 2013 when he struck on his big idea. He observed that the entire experience of scheduling meetings sucked. He started Calendly with the following intention: take the work out of scheduling meetings so that people can get more done.

But this wasn't a new idea. The meeting coordination issue has been a high-tech holy grail since *forever*. As far back as the 1980s, computing and networking platforms were laser-focused on reducing the hassle of scheduling meetings, and there was a lot of big thinking from the start. More recently, cloud computing produced an explosion of entrants. Here are just a few: TimeBridge, Tungle.me, WhenIsGood, ScheduleOnce, Plaxo, Jiffle, Congregar, Scheduly, BookFresh, Vyte, Bookeo, Meetin.gs, TimeTrade, Clara, x.ai, Motion, and Doodle. Some have gone out of business, joining the ranks of those that never made it to market. Others are still out there, with new entrants hoping AI will be the key to success.

All of these products and companies were driven by a very clear view of a problem that has plagued everyone for decades. But one thing that stymied many of them was that nobody wanted to grant third-party access to their private calendar data. BUT Calendly focused on innovation-oriented users and small companies as early adopters who cared less about the security problem. And with the rise of cloud computing, enough people were getting used to giving companies—even tiny unknown companies like Calendly—unfettered access to their personal data. Tope was in the right place at the right time.

But Tope started Calendly with no investor money, no connections, no track record of success, no customers, and no engineering talent to build it. Not an auspicious start. BUT, as he tells it, being a Nigerian-born entrepreneur means believing you can do anything.

But he wasn't an engineer, and his attempt to bring a technical cofounder into the business to build the initial product didn't work out. BUT he had just enough money to hire a Ukrainian contract development firm called Railsware.

But hiring contract developers to form the basis of a new company's engineering department is generally considered a bad idea. BUT Tope did it anyway, working hard to find a team that he says really believed in the idea and knew how to write quality code.

But just as the base Calendly product was done, Tope ran out of money. He couldn't afford to pay Railsware to add a payment mechanism. This meant he had no way to charge users. BUT, instead of stopping, he decided to make the product free, positioning it as a "freemium" release.

This is a really important part of the story. Tope ran out of money before completing the product, and he couldn't even throw the "hail Mary" pass of releasing the product and hoping that money would start flowing in from sales. This should have been a showstopper. Did he quit? Did he slow down? No. He said, "BUT hold my beer." (Full disclosure: I have no idea if Tope drinks beer.)

The freemium play was likely the crucial decision that put Calendly on the map. It led to millions of people starting to break the cycle of asking meeting attendees, "When are you available?" Followed by them replying, "I don't know, when are you available?" Followed by the suggestion, "How about Monday?" Followed by them replying, "Monday's no good. How about Tuesday?" Followed by, "Tuesday's good. What time?" And so on until everyone decides it would be easier to fling themselves from the nearest cliff at times of their own choosing.

The fact that really stands out here is that this crucial decision to offer a freemium product wasn't planned. It wasn't the result of a grand strategy. It was a 2But that answered a definitive 1But *without compromising, denying reality, or quitting*. It was a brilliant application of the Two But Rule.

But even with a freemium offering, Calendly faced a problem common to most scheduling solutions. For certain kinds of applications to be useful, both parties have to be users. This "cold start" problem usually takes vast amounts of capital and clever ways of attracting attention to reach critical mass. Uber, for example, had both plenty of money and an abundance of cleverness, allowing them to put enough drivers and passengers on their app simultaneously to make it useful for early adopters.

The cold-start problem also takes time. The fax machine took many years to reach its tipping point. The wide use of the Internet took more than 25 years after the first Internet "packet" was sent. Even these days, new social networks trying to unseat Twitter and Facebook struggle with the cold-start problem.

Calendly had neither money nor time. BUT Tope avoided the cold-start problem by designing Calendly so that it was useful without requiring invitees to be users. A Calendly user could simply generate a link showing recipients the openings on their calendar and allowing them to select a slot to book the meeting. After that, there was a good chance that the recipient would click the "join" button, turning them into a new Calendly user.

In 2014, Tope managed to add paid plans. The user base grew, and the company turned a profit in 2016. But by 2018, Calendly needed to grow past early adopters. Users wanted Calendly to have access not only to their personal calendars but also their work calendars. Imagine going to your corporate IT department and asking them to give a little company they've never heard of access to your calendar.

BUT shadow IT, the practice of employees signing up for useful services like Slack and Zoom without explicit company permission, had come into its own by 2018. Slack and other solutions were hoovering up gigabytes of internal corporate data. Employees often paid with their credit cards and expensed the cost. The dam had broken. Bureaucracies were getting used to it. Calendly made this easier by prioritizing features that IT departments wanted, like user management and compliance with enterprise security standards.

That set the stage for Calendly's growth, and Tope's past experience as an enterprise software salesperson for the likes of Perceptive, Vertafore, and EMC helped them break into the big leagues. By 2018, they started adding major customers like Marketo, Zendesk, and Zillow.

With big customers arriving, Calendly needed to expand. It needed to raise capital. But even with real users and significant growth, Tope was still on the outside looking in on the venture capital scene. He didn't fit the classic mold of a high-tech startup founder. He wasn't a Stanford or Harvard computer science dropout. He didn't party with venture capitalists. And he wasn't mentored by high-profile unicorn founders at a Silicon Valley incubator. BUT he became masterful at stretching the funds he did raise, and that led him to building a lean, disciplined organization. It also meant he didn't give away a lot of equity in the early stages of the business. When he did raise a large amount of capital, the firm was already posting $70 million in annual recurring revenue. Venture capital firms OpenView and Iconiq invested $350 million at a $3 billion valuation in 2021.

In 2022, Calendly had made it through the COVID pandemic and things were looking bright for the company, but then well-known Silicon Valley entrepreneur Sam Lessin suddenly went on Twitter and slammed the practice of sending Calendly links. BUT at least he spelled the name correctly, and instead of tanking, Calendly trended as people defended the service. New user sign-ups spiked, and soon after, *Wired* named Calendly the market leader in meeting workflow automation.

There's a lot more to the story of Calendly and Tope Awotona. According to him, he got many more things wrong on his way to getting it right. He made mistakes like not focusing on customers early enough. He sometimes let confirmation bias cloud his interpretation of experiments. But he stayed observant and learned. And it seems he got one thing right from the start: When he encountered challenges that generations of others had failed to overcome, he observed what hadn't worked before, put his but on the line against all odds, and tried it again. That's how you find the holy grail after countless others have failed.

In fairness, we forget the folks who did the same and lost. BUT, win or lose, being part of progress is an honor everyone who has started a company out of nothing shares.

When it comes to the insanely difficult world of starting a business, the ultimate BUT is this: progress depends on people willing to be innovation cannon fodder from generation to generation, both the winners and the losers. We try, try again, and then we try again. Did the winners just get lucky? No. They didn't *just* get lucky. The best of them, like Tope, learned from the past and got some things right...*and* they got lucky.

Where to Sit Your Buts

Calendly announced after the end of the pandemic that they would remain a fully remote organization. Many are making the same choice, while many others are grappling with the challenges of whether and how to return to the office.

Momentum Thinking can help build and mend relationships, and there's no better context in which to talk about relationships, dysfunction, and career displacement than the post-pandemic predicament of returning to the office...or not returning.

During the global pandemic, many workers developed a strong preference for remote work. According to a study by consulting firm McKinsey in 2022, more than 80 percent of workers took the remote option when offered. Preferences ranged from three days to a full five days a week working away from the office. By contrast, some reports suggest that as many as 50 percent of employers were requiring a full-time return to the office in 2023, with others requiring at least two days a week on site. As JP

Morgan CEO Jamie Dimon told *The Economist* in July 2023, "I completely understand why someone doesn't want to commute an hour and a half every day, totally get it. Doesn't mean they have to have a job here either."

Both the return-to-the-office and the remote-forever camps have the same deep intention. They know that great results are accomplished by high-functioning teams, and high-functioning teams are all about harmonious relationships between people who are good at what they do. Which camp you wind up in has to do with your beliefs about how best to attract great talent, keep them motivated, and foster strong co-worker relationships.

With that in mind, let's look at both approaches, starting with the return-to-the-office camp. They might articulate their intention this way: *we intend to bring everyone in our company physically back together in order to attract great, well-motivated people and empower them to do their best work by fostering productive relationships with teammates.* This option is based on the belief that team cohesion, camaraderie, collaboration, and nimbleness increase with teams that are colocated.

There's plenty to back up this perspective. Studies show that the frequency of communication between employees drops precipitously as the physical distance between them increases. Steve Jobs famously designed the Pixar headquarters to promote random physical encounters between everyone in the company. Exposure to physical cues can be essential for people to learn each other's nuanced sensibilities and build rapport. Sure, time together can lead to disagreements, squabbles, and hard feelings. But having to interact day to day means that it's harder to avoid each other and let differences fester into dysfunction.

But forcing people to return to the office after years of working from home could do more damage than good. During the pandemic, team members became accustomed to remote work. They liked the additional hours of productivity they got from not spending time commuting. BUT, if the goal is to get the benefits of physical togetherness on a regular day-to-day basis, we could avoid high traffic times by going to half days between 10 a.m. and 2 p.m.

But we don't know if four hours in the office a day really gets the benefits we're looking for, BUT we could run a test with control groups and carefully track productivity and test subject feedback.

But for many, the shortened day just doesn't work, particularly for some parents. BUT for them we can try different combinations of two or three eight-hour days a week in the office. This can help with switching costs for people who really need a full day in one location to get into the swing of a task and complete it.

But while splitting people up into different days in the office can help (and may have the unexpected side effect of increasing the number of employees supported by the same amount of office space), the problem of tribalism can still appear. People who come in on Mondays and Fridays may be prone to see each other as "us" and to refer to the Tuesday/Thursday people as "them." BUT as soon as we see this, we can implement a data-driven approach to office scheduling that balances regular in-person team interaction with the need to ensure that everyone has plenty of opportunity to mix with everyone else.

But sometimes people have to come in on days other than their regular schedule. BUT by giving everyone an online calendar where they can pick from a range of days that works for them and plan ahead—and by making reasonable allowances for people who need a stable and rigid set of on-site days every week—we can find a natural balance.

But several people moved far away during the work-from-home years. BUT according to some reports, many people regret the move and wish they could return. We have a variety of ways to make returning attractive, even if we have to tailor packages to each person's special case. When you look at the actual numbers, getting essential personnel back wouldn't break our backs financially. And we can decide on a case-by-case basis what to do about anyone who still wants to stay where they moved.

But some who are willing to return to the office may have changed their work habits and behaviors, letting interpersonal skills atrophy. For example, some may have lost the habit of keeping key team members in the loop when face-to-face discussions happen spontaneously without everyone present.

BUT we can now implement an inexpensive AI solution for each person that alerts them when it identifies email or other content that may be important to share with specific other people. This can reduce coordination and communication failures, which often lead to hard feelings. It can keep our remaining remote employees from becoming de facto outcasts, and it can even be a game-changer for on-site personnel. After all, even among people in the same building, knowledge can be sticky and unevenly shared.

But, AI systems like these are very new and may make employees feel like they're being monitored. BUT we can do a small test and design it so that the individual has sole control over their own AI and data. The AI must wait for their explicit approval before sharing anything with others.

That's just the tip of the iceberg for anyone facing a decision to require employees to return to the office. And any true 2Buts exploration depends upon the specifics of each company's situation. Still, I never had the AI-sharing idea before trying to reconcile the needs of the remaining off-site employees with the intentions of the company's return-to-the-office policy.

Now let's look at the intention of the remote-forever camp. They might articulate it this way: *we intend to have everyone work remotely and interact virtually to attract great, well-motivated people and empower them to do their best work by fostering productive relationships with teammates.*

This option is based on the belief that the convenience and flexibility offered by remote work can increase job satisfaction, productivity, and talent retention. There's evidence to support this viewpoint. Many remote workers report lower stress levels and increased productivity. Major companies have announced indefinite work-from-home policies, emphasizing the benefits of flexibility and employee well-being. And if current job postings are any indication, the remote option can attract top talent without limiting the candidate pool to those willing to live in a specific location.

But a fully remote setup can lead to employees feeling isolated, potentially harming productivity and team morale. BUT we can introduce virtual team-building activities, such as playing eSports. This approach replaces traditional in-person activities like company sports teams, providing a unique opportunity for team bonding and camaraderie.

But not everyone will be interested in online gaming, potentially excluding them from these team-building activities. BUT we can provide a range of activities to cater to various interests, such as virtual book clubs, online exercise classes, and hobby groups. This approach can help ensure that everyone feels included and part of the team.

But even with these activities, we might miss out on the spontaneous interactions that naturally occur in a physical office. These can be the spark of innovative ideas we don't want to miss. BUT we can use an AI prompter, like the one mentioned in the back-to-the-office option, to stimulate these interactions virtually. The AI can detect when notes, email, and other content produced by an employee is likely to be relevant to someone else. It can then prompt each person with, "Hey! There's someone

I think you should talk with. If you both 'swipe right,' I'll connect you." *Tinder* for teaming? What could go wrong?

But there's a risk that employees could see this AI intervention as intrusive. It could give them the sense of being monitored by the company. BUT there are modern IT methods for giving an employee complete and private control over their AI data.

But managing a remote team across multiple time zones can be the ultimate isolation problem. Traditional project management tools often fail to bridge this gap effectively. BUT we can use AI tools to create an environment that supports asynchronous communication that feels real-time and conversational. Companies such as Aimcast offer solutions that transcribe meetings and other content, decide who else should be included, and predict the right time to alert them. These systems can be designed to interpret and understand the context and content of each team member's tasks and communications, effectively acting as a teamwork coordinator between people in different time zones.

But not all discussions can be handled asynchronously. Real-time meetings are still necessary, which means inevitably someone will have to work outside normal hours. BUT we could address this by rotating meeting times, ensuring that the inconvenience of odd-hour meetings is shared. And at least we can use AI intermediation to minimize the number of times this has to occur.

There's still no definitive evidence that team dysfunction during the pandemic rose or declined during those years of isolation. But there is evidence that one type of team structure has always been particularly toxic: multiple isolated groups. The most sure-fire way to create a toxic work culture is to maintain clumps of people in separate locations. For anyone who has worked as part of an organization with people separated into different physical sites, this comes as no surprise. It doesn't take long for the team in Mumbai to start referring to the team in London as "those guys." Physical groups refer to themselves as "we" or "us." Everyone else is "them." Humans are tribal.

Well before the pandemic, a majority of organizations self-reported having dysfunctional teams, from 60 percent to as high as 75 percent, depending on the survey. Remote, hybrid, co-located—it didn't matter. Humans can have a hard time getting along no matter what their work environment looks like. Everyone has the capacity to be the pain in someone else's but. Solving for the human condition is probably best handled by writing a 10,000-page sequel to this book. Maybe we'll call it "Winning the Nobel Peace Prize in Just 10,000 Buts."

That said, habitually applying the Two But Rule can promote a more harmonious team culture, resulting in better agility and momentum. It's not a panacea, and it relies on playful professional relationships (as much as it also helps foster those relationships). But at least it doesn't rely on physical proximity to make it work.

Whether you move everyone back to the office or keep everyone remote, and especially if you have multiple in-person groups working remotely, you can help reduce dysfunction and tamp down tribalism by making sure your team develops strong Momentum Thinking habits. If you have employees returning to the office, 2But training is a good idea (especially if training comes with lunch). If you have remote teams, build the Two But Rule into your project management and virtual team tools. And if you must risk toxic tribalism by maintaining clumps of people in different locations, at least you'll know how to *hold onto your but* and pray.

14

Product and Technology Buts

When I'm not writing, I make and manage products. The two practices are more similar than you might think. Product people imagine something, turn it into a story, and then—here's the product trick—persuade others to invest their time, creativity, and resources to make it real.

People who make products for a living face complexity every day, and applying Momentum Thinking to product management is useful for anyone dealing with any kind of complex challenge.

The next three cases involve transforming social networking platforms, balancing product focus and feature creep, and dealing with the regulatory implications of artificial intelligence products.

The 2B Product Review

Before we get into the cases, a product management approach that fits well with the Two But Rule is worth a brief mention.

Ian McAllister is a product management expert known for explaining Amazon's "working backwards" approach to what he calls the *internal press release*. Before beginning work on a new project, product teams write an internal press release to be used as a touchstone to crystallize ideas and maintain alignment during development.

One way to apply the Two But Rule with this approach is to write not a press release but a product review—a product review from the near future—narrated in the voice of a future reviewer describing *both* what they liked and didn't like about the product: "I liked the price point, but I didn't like the cheap build quality. It broke in less than a week."

This prompts product and development teams to deliver the all-important 2But: "BUT we wouldn't have to sacrifice build quality to bring the cost down if we…." If you can imagine what might suck about your future product or service before you build it, then you might wind up with a superior offering in the end.

The following cases won't involve any "Two But Reviews." Still, you might find it helpful to think about the products we're going to cover, and your own projects, with this approach in mind.

Who Owns Your But Online?

These days, there's a line of software products that's turning out to be a pain in nearly everyone's *but*. Social networks. Tik Tok. Facebook. Instagram. And of course, Twitter. (Or, at the time of this writing, apparently it's...X? You know what? Let's just stick with Twitter and claim the book was already in production when we found out about the name change.)

Social networking services are rife with issues. The balance between free speech and the need to manage abuse, the desire of users to own their data versus how platforms monetize it, and the need to aggregate eyeballs versus users not wanting to be locked into a monolithic platform are just a few.

If I'm honest, I never used to care about the fact that Twitter was in control of my content and connections. If I wanted to be in control of my own content and audience, I could have set up a website easily enough.

But even those who could draw an audience to their own sites still used Twitter. Why? It was easy. It took zero effort to hop on. And once you were on, it was hard to take your eyes off the endless scroll. Eyeball aggregation. For whatever reason, Twitter drew the magic zeitgeist lottery ticket that so many product teams yearn for. Once the chain reaction of network effects started, Twitter was the place to be. And everyone knew that it was delivering something you couldn't get on your own: a place where lots of people would hear what you were saying. A global digital town square.

Then everything changed. Ownership changes, controversies, fake news, and fake news about fake news. But there was something else stirring. Everyone was talking about this crazy word: decentralization. Loosely, the word stood for the idea of building services that operate without a central authority or single point of control. For a new generation of users, the notion of decentralization was good simply "because decentralized." They even had a mantra: "Decentralize all the things." Anything centralized was to be taken out back and shot. Fair enough. Social networks changed society, and society was returning the favor by changing social networks.

To me, the word *decentralization* seems too vague. It's worth asking what the word really means in the context of social networks. Here's what I think most folks are looking for:

- We want legal ownership and control over our data, our content. Even if we store and manage that data on machines run by some company, we don't want them to own the data or use it in ways we don't explicitly authorize.

- We want to have portability. If we move our content from one platform to another, we want our followers to find us wherever we go. We want links to our content not to break after we move it. We want freedom from lock-in. And we don't want web search engines to get confused and downgrade our rankings in search results. Otherwise, people would no longer be able to find us after moving our stuff.

- We don't want to have to pay noticeably more for any of this.

But, we also want fast search and relevant content in our feeds, secure account management, and buttery-fast load times on anything from a smartphone to a web browser. We want a polished user experience, paid for by a big pool of capital backing a major brand. And when things go horribly wrong, we want to be able to hold somebody accountable to fix it, restore our data, or at least give us a refund.

If you think these two sets of requirements seem incompatible, you're right. BUT by 2023, interesting options were starting to appear. The blogging platform Substack explicitly granted writers legal ownership of their content. But the data still resided on Substack servers. BUT they added a feature to let writers use their own web domains. That addition allowed a writer to move their content off Substack and prevent links from breaking using what's called a *301 redirect*. It's wasn't easy or automatic, but it could be done with a little time and effort.

Before being moved, however, a writer's data remained under Substack's control. There was a lingering risk: Substack could, in theory, violate its agreement and censor the writer, or its systems might fail. Alternatively, the company could abruptly go out of business, causing all hosted content to vanish without a trace. Was such a scenario likely? Perhaps not, but in an era marked by growing distrust, many were seeking additional security.

However, there was a glimmer of hope on the horizon. At the time this was written, a promising new standard was being developed by the World Wide Web Consortium, with contributions from Sir Tim Berners-Lee, the inventor of the World Wide Web. This standard, known as SOLID Pods, could revolutionize user data control. If platforms like Substack or a future version of Twitter were to implement SOLID Pods, users would maintain genuine control over their data at all times. These platforms could maintain a replica of a user's data to deliver high-quality services, but if that replica were to disappear, the original data would remain safe and sound with the user.

But, this is not how Twitter or most social network platforms operate today. We may want to own, control, and move our content around as we please, but let's be honest. It costs a fair bit to run one of these platforms. Even if development and infrastructure were free, which they aren't, it's hugely expensive to establish and maintain a brand that draws billions of people to a single place. These companies want something in return for capitalizing all this. That means advertising, selling data to third parties, or high monthly fees…or all three. And the advent of data-hungry AIs like ChatGPT makes the second of these all the more attractive.

BUT in spite of this, several projects have sprung up which tout decentralization and user ownership. Particularly in the wake of Elon Musk's controversial acquisition of Twitter in early 2023, two of these, Nostr and Mastodon, gained a fair number of users seeking an alternative.

Nostr is a messaging protocol that promises to filter out disinformation and hate speech from apps that implement it. Rather than being a decentralized Twitter, the Nostr app I tried turned out to be more like "decentralized Slack," a communication channel but not a global town square. I stopped using it after about a week.

Mastodon is an open source project that has been around since 2016 and touts itself as a decentralized social network. But in my view, its decentralization is more theoretical than practical. It relies on centralized servers maintained by people you don't necessarily know. You could run a server (called an *instance*) yourself, but I suspect that most people wouldn't do that for the same reason that most people don't run their own websites.

Aside from the uncomfortable feeling I got by imagining I was storing my information on some creepy dude's server running in his mom's basement, I found the user experience to be clunky and difficult to navigate. It had limited functionality compared to Twitter. It was slow, slow, slow. And at least for me, it was a ghost town. I could hear digital crickets chirping as I waited for any sign that someone noticed my post.

BUT something interesting happened in July 2023. Meta, the company that owns Facebook and Instagram, launched a new Twitter competitor called Threads. And unlike Nostr and Mastodon, Threads attracted millions of users almost overnight by making it easy for Instagram users to add Threads to their existing accounts.

But right now Threads is as centralized as Twitter, Instagram, and Facebook. And it's way too early to tell whether this move by Meta and Mark Zuckerberg will result in sustained user growth and regular usage to topple Twitter. BUT, if Threads follows through on its public statements, it will implement the same decentralized technology standard that powers Mastodon, an open source protocol called ActivityPub, which will enable users to have direct control over their own data and reduce dependence on a central authority. But that could mean that Meta would have to relinquish the revenue streams they need to be profitable in favor of decentralized user ownership and control, right?

BUT not so fast. It's entirely possible to give users control and portability and still require a license that gives Meta rights to use the data, at least while it's on their platform. This could be hugely lucrative, especially if Meta has plans for its own AI efforts. They are going to need unfettered access to the kind of data Twitter enjoys, especially as Twitter starts to make it hard and costly for third parties like Meta to train AIs on its user's data.

If Threads prevails in the long run and does what it's promising, then it might wind up squaring the intentions of users and platform owners in true 2Buts fashion. Users will get ownership, control, and portability without giving up performance, features, accountability, or the all-important eyeball aggregation factor. Meta will get valuable data and enjoy stealing users from a rival.

The new denizens of decentralization created a mass shift in user demand. Without it, there would have been little reason for Meta or any other company to voluntarily remove their ability to lock in users. And even now, the jury is out on whether quasi-decentralized platforms like Threads (assuming they follow through) can turn a profit in the long run. At least it's a good example of how competition, driven by changes in user demand, is the ultimate decentralization…if you have the patience.

Product Feature Creep

The Two But Rule is essential for making insanely great products. But its role in the especially gnarly problem of balancing feature creep with future-proofing is worth special attention. A look at the world of specialty writing devices illustrates the issue with remarkable clarity.

I'm writing this on a reMarkable, a device that only lets me draw (and now, thanks to a new attachment, type). It's one of several examples of crowdfunded gadgets that started appearing in the years after smartphones and other devices turned our lives into a hellscape of perpetual distraction. When I work on the reMarkable, I can't check email. I can't surf the Web. And I can't get sucked into an argument on Twitter or LinkedIn about whether NFTs are the future of art or just digital Beanie Babies.

The reMarkable is a pricey little thing, and it's lost on nobody that paying more for something that deliberately does less is a perverse form of first-world problem solving. But the problem is real; distraction-free devices are a thing, and…I have one. Actually, I have two. And that's the point of this story.

Long before I discovered the wonders of the reMarkable, I was the proud owner of a Freewrite. The Freewrite lets you do just one thing: type. That's it. The original one is still a masterpiece of oddity, made of metal with satisfyingly chunky and tactile keys.

It's bulky—more luggable than laptop. It has a small Kindle-style black-and-white digital ink screen. And the original version I own has a "feature" that to some feels like a "bug." You can't go back and correct anything you previously wrote…not without backspacing your way to the correction and retyping everything after that.

Why is this a feature? Freewrite's original design philosophy is based squarely on distraction-free writing, not editing. This isn't crazy. It's a well-established principle that writing without stopping for an entire session and returning later to edit is a superior way to get the work out. But, for a generation of people who've become deeply accustomed to the freedom of inserting a cursor anywhere on the page at any time, not being able to do this is also a distraction.

Presented with, "But we're distracted by not being able to edit," Freewrite initially responded with, "BUT you can resist the urge to edit and become a better writer in the process." (This is a reasonable application of the Two But Rule.) However, over time, the need to sell more of these devices to people who were not convinced by the "you'll learn" response led to the company relenting and adding the feature.

The decision to focus on a core product philosophy is often the right thing to do, but in this case it resulted in building machines that were literally hard-wired not to allow for editing. There were no keys on the keyboard to move a cursor around. And apparently there was no way in the circuitry to map cursor moves to existing keys and simply send out a firmware update to add editing later.

So when the company added editing to later versions of the product, writers who bought the original version were stuck. The Freewrite costs hundreds of dollars. Few writers will blithely shell out that kind of money and then buy another one just to add cursor buttons.

While I was considering shelling out the dough for a new edit-friendly Freewrite, I wound up trying the reMarkable. The original version of the device focused strictly on giving people who draw or take notes with a pen a writing surface with the feel of pencil on paper (something you really miss when trying to slip an Apple Pencil around on the glass of an iPad). It had no keyboard.

Like the Freewrite, this was a very niche idea. And I wasn't someone who spent a lot of time drawing or taking paper notes. So, as much as I had admired the design and elegance of the reMarkable, I still mainly used the Freewrite.

Then in 2023, reMarkable introduced a thin leather cover for the device that hid a fold-out keyboard. And while the keys weren't chunky like the Freewrite's, typing on them was, surprisingly, an effortless joy.

But it's clear that the reMarkable was not designed to be a keyboard replacement. It's a drawing tablet first and foremost. BUT unlike the Freewrite, reMarkable had the foresight to include tiny connectors and magnetic endpoints for cases and peripherals.

That decision allowed the reMarkable to add the keyboard feature, whereas the Freewrite has zero ability to counter with a drawing surface. And reMarkable does allow editing. So now, I write (and draw) exclusively on the reMarkable, while my Freewrite collects dust.

Product developers need to stay focused on the core requirements of their product and not be distracted by feature creep, but they also need foresight to see where things could go and, wherever practical, make choices that don't box them in later.

Admittedly, that's easier said than done. Adding a keyboard to a writing surface is a lot easier than adding a drawing surface to a keyboard attached to a tiny screen.

No doubt, it is easier to make changes to software products than to physical products. But not as easy as you might think. Every decision for something in software is usually a decision against optimizing for something else.

It's clear that reMarkable had made decisions in the original software on the device that did not contemplate—and certainly didn't optimize for—adding a keyboard-based user experience. BUT they made the code open source, allowing easier discovery of problems, greater opportunity for third party integrations, and more flexibility in general.

The Freewrite team made great, focused product decisions. But change came and boxed them in anyway. Navigating between future-proofing and optimizing for today involves a lot of luck, especially for hardware products.

The same goes for services, as we see today with Uber and Lyft. To date, Lyft has remained focused on ridesharing, while

Uber risked losing focus by adding UberEats in 2014. Many see Uber outperforming Lyft today, but in an alternative universe where the pandemic never happened, it's possible that the story would be about how Lyft overtook Uber through better focus on core competencies.

There are no right answers—except in hindsight—but taking a little time periodically to apply the Two But Rule can help spot change coming and consider options.

In the end, what reMarkable showed is that sometimes product developers and designers have the option to say, "Don't build that feature now, BUT don't build our current product in a way that would make it hard to add it later." It doesn't work in all cases, but when it does, it's...*remarkable*.

Regulating AI

New products and technologies often bring with them a Pandora's box of new challenges and complexities. The Two But Rule can help more thoroughly address these secondary problems, ideally before they get out of control.

We've been talking a lot about artificial intelligence in this book, and I hope I've made a good case for why that is. The human tendency toward bounded rationality and susceptibility to mental fatigue makes rigorous application of the Two But Rule a big ask for everyday use. It's fortunate that AI, which can effectively reduce friction and extend the process of Momentum Thinking, is exploding in popular use right now.

But, there's a big problem with AI that deserves a proper 2Buts treatment itself: AI regulation. BUT, we got this.

Let's take a look at an argument about AI regulation that appeared in a popular podcast in 2023 between some of the tech industry's most well-known commentators: Chamath Palihapitiya, David Sacks, David Friedberg, and Jason Calacanis of the

All-In Podcast. In episode 124, the podcast tackled the issue of regulating the development and proliferation of artificial intelligence. What follows is a quick summary.

Chamath argued that AI must be regulated because there are clear and present dangers to unchecked proliferation. He suggested that a regulatory body, similar to the Federal Drug Administration, should be created to do it.

David Sacks and David Friedberg argued that it's too early to know how to regulate, that it wouldn't effectively stop proliferation, and that government intervention typically slows innovation and drives it underground or overseas.

Jason kept the conversation rolling and encouraged the others to square their points of view. (Jason is a natural practitioner of Momentum Thinking.)

Everyone agreed that like it or not, regulation is coming.

AI regulation is a huge, gnarly problem. It's full of tricky balance points. It's the kind of problem that defies absolute solutions. And we'll be grappling with it until our new AI overlords take over. (Just kidding…at least I think I'm kidding.)

If you watch to the whole *All-In* episode, you'll notice where the conversation starts to go circular, repeating points and counterpoints. This happens when even smart, well-informed people embrace only one of their buts at a time. And if you happen to find the tweet proposing AI regulation that Chamath posted before the podcast, you'll see a ton of reactionary 1Buts in the thread of replies…mixed with the weird evangelism and ad hominem attacks that make Twitter such a joy.

With this in mind, let's apply the Two But Rule to the concerns raised by David Sacks and David Friedberg about AI regulation.

To prepare for this case, I spent hours researching the AI regulation topic. Then I reviewed ideas with colleagues who know a thing or two about the subject. And then I consulted the best Momentum Thinker of all time: ChatGPT. Yep, there's nothing like talking to an AI about regulating AI. Presenting all the different threads here would make for a very long chapter. So I cherry-picked a few.

Issue 1: AI regulation won't keep pace with innovation, BUT maybe it would if we employed AI-driven regulatory tools that learn and adapt at the same pace. Here's the argument: the best way for regulators to keep pace with AI is to use AI in the development, monitoring, and modification of AI regulation. Anyone using large language models like ChatGPT frequently these days can see the sense of this. It's reasonable to believe that AI systems can be trained to monitor progress and recommend regulatory updates in accordance with high-level regulatory principles. It's even reasonable to believe that doing this wouldn't be a herculean feat, given the current state of the technology.

But an AI watchdog won't work, because:

- Relying heavily on AI-driven tools for regulation might introduce vulnerabilities, as bad actors could potentially target these tools to bypass regulatory measures or manipulate the regulatory process.

- A watchdog AI can monitor only what it can see, so this leaves out advances developed in secret.

- Even if the AI watchdog is fast on the draw to identify necessary changes, the human regulatory system is woefully inadequate to react in a timely way to the recommendations.

BUT these issues can be addressed by:

- Making the watchdog system principally open source and offering a compellingly large international "bug bounty"—funded by the widest possible set of governments and other institutions—that can encourage people to continuously identify problems, vulnerabilities, and logic issues.

- Offering huge rewards on any information leading to the discovery of secret AI research.

- Creating a regulatory "high-speed lane" within limited, well-defined subjects. While it's not plausible that we can turn government bodies into speed demons, it's a well-established practice to "run slow" on creating and promulgating statutes while running faster on specific regulatory rulemaking and enforcement. Speed and confidence can be enhanced by writing clear limits to the latitude that the regulators working with the AI watchdog have to make changes.

Issue 2: Regulation will slow down innovation, BUT maybe it wouldn't if we created an open sandbox testing service. Here's the argument: sandboxing AI can provide a controlled environment for testing and evaluating AI applications, ensuring that any potential risks, biases, or harmful behaviors are identified and addressed before any AI is released to the public. Chamath suggested this in the podcast. This approach might improve the safety and trustworthiness of AI systems and minimize the risks associated with deploying untested or potentially harmful AI applications.

But a sandbox may not work, because:

- Sandboxing AI might slow down the development and deployment process, potentially stifling innovation and limiting the benefits of advancements. It's easy to imagine a bottleneck forming as multiple projects try to get access to the sandbox.

- Sandboxing could create a false sense of security, as AI applications might behave differently in a controlled environment compared to real-world situations. This could lead to unforeseen issues and vulnerabilities.

BUT these issues can be addressed by:

- Developing an open standard for sandbox testing and providing subsidized compute resources to providers of sandbox services so that there's a diverse and market-driven set of options for AI developers and researchers of all sizes and types to use quickly, easily, and at a price that they can afford.
- Monitoring AI applications after they have been released from the sandbox and feeding learnings back into testing models and standards.

Issue 3: It takes only one failure for an AI that isn't aligned with the interests of humanity to break out, cause major damage, and defy containment after the fact. BUT we could make "trust nothing unsigned" the Internet's default setting.

Here's the argument: It's true that our best measures to prevent an artificial general intelligence from breaking out and wreaking havoc may not be enough. And it seems likely that even one case could be ruinous and hard to contain. BUT it's possible to flip protocols, routers, and Internet-connected endpoints like web browsers from assuming content and code are permitted to assuming that no content or code is safe or real unless digitally signed by verified creators. This could become commonplace quickly, particularly if deep fake proliferation becomes so widespread that nobody trusts anything they see on the Web. It would make sense for browsers to add the option to filter for signed content initially, making it the default over time. If this happened, any transmissions coming from an AI that didn't generate a signature proving it passed sandbox testing would be filtered, and security organizations could be alerted to track down the "rogue" AI.

The notion of "flipping the Internet" to filter out content that doesn't have a digital signature from a verified creator might seem far-fetched, but it is not unheard of. You may not have noticed, but at some point a few years ago most websites flipped from the old HTTP protocol to the more secure HTTPS standard. Web browser makers like Mozilla and Google are constantly evaluating new standards, and while it seems to take forever to reach consensus and implement new standards, sometimes an urgent need can turbocharge the process. That urgent need is upon us as the world grapples with the mass incursion of deep fakes that can lead us to believe falsehoods and question verifiable truths. The only way for us to trust that what we see is coming from a source of truth is for the Internet to trust nothing that isn't digitally signed.

But flipping to "trust nothing unsigned" won't work, because:

- Implementing the default filtering of unsigned content might inadvertently block legitimate content that hasn't been signed, leading to reduced access to valuable information and resources.
- Default filtering could be seen as a form of censorship, raising concerns about Internet freedom and the potential for misuse or abuse by governments or other entities.

BUT these issues can be addressed by:

- Implementing a user-friendly mechanism in browsers and apps for reporting false positives and allowing users to flag and automatically unblock valuable resources that may have been inadvertently filtered. This feedback system would enable continuous improvement of the filtering mechanism.
- Ensuring transparency in the filtering process by providing open source tools and fast processes for generating and managing the necessary signatures. This can be further secured

against inappropriate censorship through privacy-preserving techniques like Zero Knowledge cryptography, which can allow a browser to pass the content without knowing anything about the identity of the signer other than the fact that it's an approved entity. This can help maintain trust and prevent accusations of censorship or misuse of the filtering system.

Wikipedia lists numerous global and national initiatives addressing AI regulation. I found them to be mainly a series of high-level "we shoulds": "We should make sure AI doesn't discriminate" or "We should work together to ensure AI aligns with human interests." These statements are just begging to be 1Butted to death. And as you would expect, even a single application of "but that won't work, BUT it would if…" is hard to find.

The more I look around at the big problems ahead, the more I notice how we limit ourselves in the ways we explore them—too afraid to tell someone that their idea has flaws on one hand and too rushed or lazy to provide more than a single "but that won't work" on the other.

It was a refreshing experience exploring this topic and taking the time to iterate through the Two But Rule on it, even though we had room only for a few iterations here. That said, just as I couldn't help thinking that there were a lot more buts to discover after listening to the *All-In* episode, the hope is that you'll have the same reaction to this and add more buts to this important conversation.

Who knows? Maybe if enough of us do it, eventually world leaders, grappling with AI regulation and other gnarly issues, will start employing the Two But Rule themselves. It might help them make sure that the many challenges facing humanity don't wind up kicking their buts.

15

Buts in Conflict

Whether it's battles over territory, budget disputes, or food fights in the cafeteria, humans have a penchant for conflict. It's either a symptom of 1Butism or a sign of how little time we spend trying to understand and honor what's behind each other's intentions.

Let's look at two cases of conflict, one from the earliest days of democracy and one pulled from today's headlines.

Solon, Father of Buts

This book wouldn't be complete without a case on how the Two But Rule can be applied to political and social conflict. Finding the right case left me with a classic 2Buts problem. I looked at the war in Ukraine, the conflict over the U.S. election of 2020, Brexit, the Arab Spring, the Troubles in Ireland, the partition of India and Pakistan, World War II, World War I, and even the

French Revolution. But every topic I considered was likely to focus stakeholders on the deficiencies of my research rather than considering how they might apply Momentum Thinking to current conflicts. BUT, it struck me that there might be a case from so long ago that all the combatants are long dead and their direct connection to anyone's current interests long forgotten. But I'm not an expert in ancient history. BUT it happens that my best college friend from UC Berkeley, Dr. Duane March, has a PhD in ancient history and Mediterranean archaeology. It's a degree, I should add, that typically involves acquiring at least six years of postgraduate study and proficiency in two ancient languages.

So I looked him up and gave him a tough assignment: find a story about a conflict that was, or could have been, resolved in a superior way by using Momentum Thinking. I added the extra challenge that the story needed to be clearly relatable to conflicts we're grappling with today. He didn't disappoint. The story he told comes from Athens, the birthplace of democracy.

Around 600 BCE, Athens was in the middle of a crisis. Faith in legal and political institutions was at an all-time low. Society was divided into self-interested groups with little trust—and a lot of animosity—between them. Armed conflict was a real possibility. Sound familiar?

There were four main stakeholders. The Eupatrids were the old, traditional families of Attica, the region surrounding Athens. In 600 BCE, they were the only ones who were allowed to occupy state offices or serve as judges. They were, by all accounts, clannish and tended to favor their own people in disputes with other members of society. They held a lot of land and maintained a patron-client relationship with their lower-status neighbors, often trading services for protection. Effectively this meant that Athens in 600 BCE was run as something between an aristocracy and a mafia state.

The Thetes were poor farmers. They had to borrow seed, using their land and bodies as collateral. A bad harvest could leave them in debt, and if they couldn't pay it off, they could be sold into slavery. They had no political power.

Hoplites made up much of the military class. They were typically farmers who did well enough to afford weapons and armor. Even though they formed the bulk of the Athenian infantry, they had almost no political power, and bad luck with their harvests could land them in the same cycle of debt and slavery as the Thetes.

Then there was the merchant class, who engaged in commerce that flourished all over the Mediterranean. They were wealthy enough to buy weapons and armor, and some could afford horses and serve in the Athenian cavalry. In spite of their growing economic and military significance, they couldn't hold office and had little influence over state policies, even the ones that directly impacted trade.

In 632 BCE, an Athenian aristocrat named Cylon appealed to the Hoplites to back him as an absolute monarch, a *tyrannos* (tyrant). He seized the Acropolis and nearly succeeded in gaining control over Athens, but in the end he failed to gather enough support and was forced to flee.

The incident made it clear to the Eupatrids that a tyrant could rise if things got bad enough for the Hoplites and the other factions. And they saw it happen in other surrounding cities, including Corinth, Sicyon, Samos, Naxos, Megara, and Miletus.

By 595 BCE, everyone knew something had to change. Yeah, that's 37 years after the Cylon uprising, but hey, they didn't have iPhones, and things moved at a different pace. The Eupatrids didn't want to see the rise of tyranny, but they wanted to retain their political influence, social privileges, and wealth. The merchant class wanted the same privileges as the Eupatrids, particularly to counter their monopoly in legal disputes, but the Eupatrids obviously didn't want to share power. Both Hoplites and Thetes wanted debt relief, freedom from the threat of slavery, and an equal playing field in legal disputes. But, obviously this was seen by the other stakeholders as a zero-sum game that could be solved only by their losing power and privilege.

They were at an impasse, BUT because virtually nobody wanted to descend into tyranny, they struck a grand bargain and agreed to abide by the decrees of a single person. In 594 BCE, they elected a guy named Solon to be Archon, the leading executive of the state in charge of making new laws. Only a Eupatrid could be named Archon, but that risked the other factions rejecting the choice and not abiding by the agreement. BUT Solon garnered wide support and trust, because he came from a less powerful family and had distinguished himself as a just and fair leader.

Solon's new laws forbade the enslavement of Athenian citizens as payment for debt, and he had the state buy the freedom of already-enslaved citizens. He abolished all current debt and relieved all property from current mortgages. He even wrote a poem about it: "The mortgage-stones that covered the land were removed by me; the land that was slave is free." Presumably he was a better leader than poet. (Full disclosure: Dr. March points out that Solon was considered to be a great poet, but at least in translation from the original Greek, he's no Maya Angelou.)

He created a citizen assembly that admitted even the poorest Athenians. The assembly could elect officials, hear debate on issues, and approve laws. He established a court in which all citizens qualified as jurors, and he divided the population into four classes based solely on wealth. (This might not seem like a terrific option to modern eyes, but it was a big deal then.) And while he was at it, he standardized weights and measures, which helped protect everyone from cheating. Not a bad start.

But the Eupatrids still weren't happy about wealthy merchants rising in status and gaining access to political offices.

BUT, because they were all very wealthy, the Eupatrids still maintained a virtual monopoly on ultimate power. And this arrangement gave the merchants hope that their growing wealth could turn into political power over time. This prevented them from backing a tyrant.

The Hoplites still wanted to weaken the Eupatrids and become war leaders, which the other groups feared could lead to a military coup. BUT, Hoplites could now serve in many offices, their lands were free of mortgages, and they now had a direct influence on the assembly. They also could protect their interests in the new citizen court.

The Thetes still wanted Eupatrid lands broken up and distributed to the people. But that was never going to happen so long as the aristocracy and other groups remained. That decision would have led to civil war. BUT, Solon wiped out their debts, freed poor farmers from mortgages, and gave everyone direct influence on state business through the assembly and the new citizen court.

Solon's law wasn't the kind of lazy compromise we see, even to this day, in political gamesmanship. He literally changed the game. While many of the buts Solon handled are lost to history, he left more bad poetry that establishes him as one of the great but-heads of antiquity:

> *"Such power I gave the people as was right, I took nothing away and gave in addition. Those that possessed great wealth and high station, my counsel protected from disgrace. Before both sides I held my mighty shield, and allowed neither to infringe the rights of the other."*

Solon recognized that his laws were not universally popular, and there was a risk of them being eroded or rescinded. BUT Athenians had sworn to uphold the laws unless he himself changed them. So after the new laws were approved, Solon got his *but* out of there and left Athens for a 10-year trip around the known world so that he couldn't be induced to make changes. That maneuver was such a brilliant application of the Two But Rule that it might warrant naming Solon the Father of Buts. We can leave that decision for the soon-to-be established But-Head Assembly.

But…yeah, this wasn't the end of the buts. Sadly, the Athenian infighting didn't end. Humans, once they go tribal, have very stubborn buts. In the coming years, they failed to elect a Chief Archon four times. (The lack of an Archon, by the way, was called *anarchy*.) Then, in 546 BCE, a Eupatrid named Peisistratus seized power in a military coup. He and his sons ruled as tyrants for the next 36 years.

BUT, while the tyrannical dictatorship wasn't avoided, something unexpected happened. It turns out that Peisistratus was a big fan of Solon. (Some sources suggest they might have been lovers.) So in spite of establishing a military dictatorship, he largely upheld Solon's laws. In time, this led to the formation of the democratic institutions Athens is known for today.

Was conflict avoided? No. Was the march to Athenian democracy interrupted by infighting, anarchy, and dictatorship? Yes. But, the steps Solon took to balance the many buts of Athenian society in his time led to a flourishing of democracy later. To paraphrase both Mahatma Ghandi and Martin Luther King, Jr., there have been tyrants, and for a time they seem invincible, BUT the long arc of history bends toward freedom, equality, and justice.

Big Government's Budget Buts

Now let's leap from the birthplace of democracy to the present. You'd think that a legislative body composed of two houses, like the United States Congress, would inherently embrace the notion of the Two But Rule. You'd think that for every proposal or bill there would be a lot of Momentum Thinking going on.

A lot of "But that won't work, BUT it would if…" conversations. Maybe on a good day this really does happen—at least among staffers off-camera. Usually, though, what we see is a lot of 1Butism: circular arguments that go nowhere and result in combatants just repeating talking points until we all start to contemplate the merits of anarchy.

My buddy ChatGPT and I have been looking into cases of Congress getting stuck in circular arguments. We started talking about the U.S. debt ceiling "crisis" of 2023, when one political party spent more than five months blocking the authorization of borrowing to cover what the government had already spent.

I'm not going to go into the whole backstory about what the debt ceiling is, how it came to be a thing, or why we seem perennially compelled to play financial Russian roulette with it. But for a sizzling account of the history, check out *Debt Limit Through The Years* by the Bipartisan Policy Center. It's a page-turner. Here are some highlights:

1939: The first U.S. debt ceiling is set at $45 billion.

1957: Congress waits six months to approve a new debt limit as a way to force the Eisenhower administration to constrain defense spending.

1979: After nearly causing a default, Congress allows budget resolutions to increase the debt ceiling without a special vote.

1982: The federal debt limit is codified into law and later increased to $2.1 trillion.

1982 to the present: The debt limit increases 39 times, with multiple cases of partisan brinkmanship taking the United States close to default. It now stands at more than $31 trillion.

Here's the strange thing about the debt ceiling. If you've listened to any sitting president during any of these made-up and unnecessary crises, raising the debt limit is about paying for things we've already bought. It's about paying the minimum fee on the national credit card, so to speak.

But whichever party is in the minority when it comes time to cover those debts tends to use the moment to get really serious about how the government is spending too much...or at least spending too much on the things they don't like.

Why don't they get serious during the normal budget process and avoid spending more than the previous limit allows or simply agree to raise limits then? One big reason is this: the United States defaulting on its debt would throw the world into financial Armageddon, and that makes for good TV. It's a chance for the opposition to get a ton of airtime and attention on the spending issues they care about. The problem is that this clown show has already resulted in taking things too far, twice causing a downgrade of the U.S. credit rating.

I asked ChatGPT about how we might avoid all this. I also asked some humans—they're still marginally useful and will make excellent companions in the very nice cage ChatGPT is building for me. We came up with the usual suspects—from bipartisan budget reform to public education, tying debt ceiling increases directly to spending decisions and encouraging more cooperation through campaign finance reform.

The full transcript of that chat ran to dozens of 1Buts and 2Buts. Nothing seemed to address the deep motivation of getting eyeballs for the opposition. So we dug deeper on that specifically, which led to ideas about getting more media attention on fiscal debates and town halls, creating a "fiscal responsibility award," and various forms of media partnerships.

But none of these was likely to get U.S. Congress members the level of focused media attention that they're enjoying now from the debt ceiling drama. BUT, it struck us that maybe we could add some sizzle if we applied some of the techniques of reality TV shows, including shows like *American Idol*…maybe even have viewers donate to congressional campaigns based on who "won" a given issue.

But we quickly identified problems with that, including the fact that reality TV thrives on polarizing behavior that wouldn't help find positive solutions. These budget negotiations are often confidential, and people might vote and donate along purely party lines, regardless of the merits of the arguments.

BUT we thought we might solve those issues by including tricks employed by the show *The Masked Singer* to hide party affiliations. We even thought of producing the whole show from generative AI to avoid taxing Congress members' limited acting chops.

And then…it all came together. It struck me that we could feature young people applying to become congressional interns. We could use follow-cam footage and other techniques to create drama. ChatGPT obliged with a complete Netflix showrunner's proposal. Yeah, no kidding!

And so, we humbly present for your consideration: *Budget Wars*!

Title: Budget Wars.

Format: Reality TV/political drama.

Logline: Future political leaders confront the drama and complexity of fiscal policy, embodying the roles of anonymous Congress members in a riveting blend of competition, debate, and behind-the-scenes action.

Episodes: 12 episodes, 60 minutes each.

Overview: In Budget Wars, ambitious congressional intern candidates are plunged into the heart of American fiscal policy, representing anonymous Congress members. The show blends traditional debate with personalized narrative arcs, backstage coaching, and real-world interactions, culminating in an audience vote that supports the party's campaign fund of choice.

Episode Structure:

Intern Proxy Proposal Presentation (10 minutes): Intern candidates, coached by industry experts, present fiscal policy proposals on behalf of anonymous Congress members.

Backstage Coaching and Comments (10 minutes): America's Got Talent–style backstage footage shows experts providing feedback and strategy advice, interspersed with contestants' reactions and reflections.

Intern Proxy Counter-Proposal and Debate (20 minutes): Interns critique and improve upon the proposals, with audience voting opening at the conclusion of this segment.

Follow-Cam Action (15 minutes): We follow contestants around Washington, providing a glimpse into their interactions, challenges, and breakthroughs. This segment captures the drama and personal journey of each contestant, serving as a compelling narrative thread throughout the series.

Results and Reveal (5 minutes): Votes are tallied, the winning team is announced, and the real Congress members are revealed. The audience can then choose to contribute to the RNC or DNC in honor of the winning team.

Engagement and Education: *Budget Wars provides a unique and engaging approach to understanding fiscal policy, bringing viewers closer to the political process.*

Youth Perspective: *The show brings a fresh perspective to politics by showcasing the viewpoints and journeys of young intern candidates.*

Interactivity: *Audience voting and the opportunity to contribute to campaign funds make the show a participatory experience.*

Target Audience: *Politically engaged viewers of all ages, as well as fans of reality competition shows and political dramas.*

Marketing Strategy: *Social media engagement, behind-the-scenes content, and expert commentary to maintain viewer interest and deepen understanding of fiscal policy.*

Potential Challenges: *Balancing the complexity of fiscal policy with engaging storytelling, ensuring accurate representation of the representatives' views, managing the ethical implications of the competition and donation aspects.*

Conclusion: *Budget Wars is a unique and compelling blend of political debate, reality competition, and personal drama. By humanizing the complex world of fiscal policy, the show promises to be a standout addition to any network's lineup.*

—Compiled from ChatGPT-generated
content based on multiple inputs

Did we solve the budget crisis and end congressional brinkmanship for all time with a reality TV show? No, probably not. But Momentum Thinking isn't always about directly solving the problem you set out to address. It's about using that problem as the starting point of a journey and seeing where it takes you.

Now…who is going to produce this show?!? (No, seriously. *Budget Wars* is must-see TV.)

CHAPTER

16

Saving the World...with Your But

I hope you're feeling good. You should. We've just flexed our buts on some gnarly topics. And I'd like to think that you've been testing your Momentum Thinking skills on your own challenges along the way. Our buts should now be so toned and sculpted that they could, indeed, appear in a Marvel movie.

We're just in time, because like any Marvel superhero, we're getting the signal to save the day. Whole books could be written applying the Two But Rule to the many scourges of climate change, economic collapse, the next pandemic, nuclear/meteoric/ zombie apocalypses, *mass hysteria*! But for now, we're going to look at just two challenges: balancing competing issues in wind energy and getting plastic pollution under control. By the way, make sure to drink a protein shake or something before tackling

the plastic case. It's a big one! And then we will have arrived
at the end of the book! (I know. I know. You want more, right?
Me too, but I have to leave some cases for the sequels.)

Windy Buts

The otherwise harmonious worlds of environmental conservation and clean energy generation have a dilemma. The latter is
building a ton of wind turbines that are killing between one and
six million birds a year in the United States alone. Even though
there are bigger things contributing to avian mortality, that's a
lot of dead birds. And clean energy people don't want bird blood
on their hands.

In the late 2000s, the U.S. Fish and Wildlife Service wanted
to protect endangered bird species, including the Red-Tailed
Hawk and the Golden Eagle. Wind energy developers wanted to
continue expanding wind farms to produce clean energy and
combat climate change. That's not a bad goal, but doing so without a solution for the bird fatality problem could have led to legal
action and fines, not to mention providing a potent argument for
those opposing wind farms. BUT engineers found that the place-
ment and spacing of vertically oriented wind turbines could significantly reduce bird fatalities. This led to the development of
vertical axis wind turbines.

But there were a bunch of physical and energy efficiency
issues with their designs. They couldn't take advantage of wind
direction, and they took an efficiency hit because half of the blade
system was always moving against the wind. The vertical orienta-
tion also limited how high the towers could be built and how
much wind had to be present to get the contraption moving.
They also produced a lot of vibration and structural stress, leading to higher maintenance costs. BUT some suggest that the

notion of vertical blades led to the development of *bladeless* wind turbines, a new technology that promises to generate energy without rotating blades.

Bladeless turbines use vertically oriented strands of resonating material that capture wind energy from all directions. They have no moving parts and are cheaper than traditional wind turbines to produce. They don't have the bird kill problem, and they are quiet, making them preferable for both environmentalists and neighbors. But, while they are increasing in efficiency, they are still as much as 30 percent less efficient than bladed turbines, and they require higher wind speeds to start generating energy. BUT, this is a relatively new technology, and teams are making significant improvements. And because they take up less space and are cheaper to produce, bladeless wind farms could produce more total power per square mile than traditional wind farms. By 2030, an estimated 1,500 traditional wind turbines will be nearing end-of-life. It's possible that a bladeless alternative could replace them.

Innovators working on wind energy and conservation didn't accept the false choice between deadlock and unacceptable compromise. They didn't say, "6 million dead birds is too much, BUT 500,000 would be acceptable." Instead, they reoriented their buts and stacked them vertically, finding a potential win-win in the process. It's yet to be seen how effective and widely adopted this new technology will be. And there are still many buts to be handled. Nevertheless, the work goes on, and the intention of generating clean energy without disregarding environmental conservation has not been abandoned for lazy 1But or 0But options. Maybe it has something to do with working on a form of nearly inexhaustible power that makes these folks so good at sustaining the iterative process of the Two But Rule and playing the long game.

Plastic Buts

I hope you aren't *winded* from that short case, because it's time to clean up some plastic.

Between 4 and 12 million metric tons of plastic enter the world's oceans every year. It can take hundreds of years to completely biodegrade. And as plastic breaks down, it becomes nasty bits of microplastic. Microplastics now show up in everything from plankton to humans…even human placentas. Catch plastic before it reaches the ocean, and you have a better chance of getting it out of the environment before it breaks down. But once it's in the ocean, much of it is destined to become an unrecoverable, pervasive part of the ecosystem.

We're still learning the specific harms all this plastic is doing to marine life (and to ourselves), but it doesn't take a marine biologist to understand that this is a problem that should be prioritized right up there with getting Elon Musk off the planet and resolving Taylor Swift's war with Ticketmaster.

Research chemist Captain Charles Moore made combatting ocean pollution his life's priority. He's famous for discovering and studying a giant mass of human-made trash swirling around the North Pacific known as the Great Pacific Garbage Patch. It's about twice the size of Texas (620,000 square miles) and home to a lot of plastic, more than a trillion pieces. It's one of five known accumulation zones in the world's oceans.

When science reporter Kate Bieberdorf asked Captain Moore in 2023 what he thought we could do to stop plastic pollution and clean up the mess, the man who had devoted his life, career, and fortune to the mission said simply, "Cleanup is an impossibility, and stopping it is also impossible."

That's a pretty definitive 1But. Let's see where the Two But Rule takes us.

Before we continue, I should tell you that this is a long case, the longest one in this book. The landfill full of buts we're about to pick through can really wear you out. I've added some pauses and a few jokes here and there to make this story easier to digest. (Easier than a tasty hunk of plastic.) With that said, let's get ourselves up to our buts in plastic.

Here's our intention: Massively reduce plastic entering the ocean so that it stops being a factor in the destruction of the marine ecosystem, which provides a significant portion of the world's oxygen and much of the human food supply.

But massively reducing the flow of plastic into the ocean feels overwhelming, because it's hard to know where to start. BUT there's enough data today to pick a starting place where specific actions can have the greatest impact.

Let's look at the different ways we can reduce the flow of plastic to the ocean.

- We can catch the plastic before it reaches the ocean.
- We can reclaim perfectly sorted plastic waste immediately at the point of consumption.
- We can magically make the plastic disappear after it reaches the sea or transform it into a substance that won't hurt the ecosystem. (Crazy, yes, but stay with me.)
- We can stop making and using plastic. (Well, that's definitely crazy talk, right? Stay tuned.)

Let's take a look at the first option. Around 60 percent of plastic pollution gets to the ocean by way of rivers. Eliminating that source would massively reduce ocean plastic pollution. Definitely a good start.

But removing plastics from rivers isn't practical, because there are hundreds of thousands of rivers covering millions of miles.

BUT recent studies show that about 80 percent of river-borne plastic enters the ocean through only a thousand rivers. If those figures are correct, we could prevent roughly 50 percent of new plastic flowing to the ocean by catching and removing it at these specific locations. A thousand sites might seem like a lot, but it's a finite, workable number.

But the task of finding and physically removing plastic from these rivers is still daunting and expensive. We're talking about literally millions of miles of water under the jurisdiction of many different countries. BUT we can reduce the problem of finding the plastic by erecting filters to catch the plastic near estuaries, the river mouths that flow to the sea.

But that won't work for several reasons. First, there are many types of river estuaries, and plastics are known to inhabit water strata all the way from the riverbed to the surface. To effectively catch and remove the plastic, we would have to create filters that covered the entire breadth and depth of the river while allowing the water to flow freely. Otherwise, the water would simply overflow the barrier or create a new opening to the ocean.

Second, river estuaries are complex and diverse. Building custom filter barriers for each type would significantly increase complexity and cost.

Third, even if we could erect inexpensive, effective filter barriers that let water flow freely, they would disrupt fish and other marine creatures and would certainly hinder boats and other maritime traffic in and out of the river. That's a nonstarter for any navigable waterway, and some of the most polluted estuaries that need cleaning are also ones that provide shipping access to ports.

BUT what if we could erect a filter barrier that entirely covered almost any type of river with a simple and reasonably inexpensive mechanism to deploy and maintain, one that didn't disrupt marine life or navigation?

It turns out that a company in the Netherlands has done exactly this. The Great Bubble Barrier company has built what it calls a Bubble Barrier and demonstrated that it can collect as much as 86 percent of river-borne plastic before it reaches the sea.

According to the company, the curtain works by pumping air through a reasonably simple and inexpensive perforated tube placed on the bottom of the waterway. This creates an upward current, which brings the plastics to the surface. By placing the tube diagonally in the river, the natural flow of the water directs the plastics into a catchment system at the riverbank. The Bubble Barrier allows fish to pass, doesn't hinder ship traffic, and covers the entire width and depth of the waterway.

The first long-term bubble curtain was installed in Amsterdam in November 2019. In 2022, the first bubble curtain to be implemented in an estuary was placed in de Oude Rijn, in Katwijk. The company now has plans to roll out the solution to more rivers in Europe and Asia.

Problem solved, right?

But this is just a small implementation, and we need 1,000 estuaries covered as soon as possible. And even in the European Union there are as yet no comprehensive regulations driving river plastic monitoring or cleanup.

BUT, the Great Bubble Barrier's CTO, Philip Ehrhorn, points out that they are already using general pollution regulations and initiatives to drive momentum. There's active interest from municipalities to reduce the tourism-killing ugliness of floating debris. Plastic debris also fouls waterway management systems and hydroelectric power plants. That's a start as plastic regulation catches up.

But the company reports that an impediment to faster deployment is the complicated governance structures around waterways. It's not always clear who has responsibility for this kind of cleanup at the river mouth. Who should pay for it? Who should collect the revenue from selling or processing the waste? Who should be responsible for maintenance? BUT the company has developed a service to help municipalities navigate these political and jurisdictional waters, and it's starting to work. They have expanded to advocating that river plastic be defined and included in the UN Global Plastics Treaty.

But there are limits to the kinds of rivers the Bubble Barrier can support right now. Anne Marieke Eveleens, a cofounder of the Great Bubble Barrier, says, "Some port rivers can be too deep, and it's difficult if there is riverbed dredging multiple times a year." BUT a new study has revealed that the majority of river plastic is entering the ocean from small and medium-sized rivers where the Bubble Barrier has already proven effective. And they are still pushing the limits of their technology.

But even if we immediately were able to implement solutions like the Great Bubble Barrier, there's still a big problem. We don't know what to do with all the plastic we catch. And a lot of other kinds of trash and material can wind up in the catchment system. Furniture, mattresses, clothing, teddy bears, diapers, and even refrigerators and tires. A lot of floating organic matter can also get caught, including wood, weeds, and dead animals.

Sorting through all this stuff and sending each type of waste material to an effective and ethically responsible recycling facility is another daunting proposition.

There are two BUTs here. First, unlike other filtering systems that use skimmers and grates, the Bubble Barrier doesn't tend to get fouled as much with big heavy stuff like refrigerators, mattresses, and the occasional dead moose. Second, what if there were a way to automate sorting, inexpensively convert the plastic and other materials that enter the catchment, and turn all the waste into profitable, useful, or at least harmless byproducts right there on site?

Remember Elon Musk's fuzzy but, imagining a "magic wand for turning atoms into rockets" that led to 3D printing SpaceX Raptor engines? What if we could reverse the idea and turn junk back into atoms: pure and profitable recycled plastic base ingredients, environmentally safe byproducts, energy production, and materials that the local community near the collection site could turn into products? What if we could do that without having to incur the expense of transporting it from the river collection site?

This *fuzzy but* is admittedly a bit of science fiction, but it's still a legitimate application of Momentum Thinking. And there are examples of on-site reclamation systems that exist today. There's an AI optical system that, connected to a high-speed air-jet, identifies different kinds of plastics and blows them to different bins at astonishing speed. There's a company in Africa that grinds up all kinds of plastic and bakes it into construction bricks that are virtually indestructible, water resistant, and up to 40 percent cheaper than traditional building material.

AI is getting in on the act, as you'd expect. Researchers at the University of Texas at Austin used an AI neural network in 2022 to look at 19,000 proteins and discovered three combinations that generated a highly active enzyme that broke down a plastic tray within 48 hours. They call it the Super Enzyme, and it can retrieve 94.9 percent of the material needed to make new plastic products. This can reduce the need to make new plastic from fossil fuels. The output is pure liquid ingredients that are easy to transport. Imagine a river catchment system that dispensed plastic "liquid gold" like tapping a maple tree for syrup.

But not all plastics work in this process, so we need to sort them, and that can be expensive, time-consuming human labor. BUT Sweden's Chalmers University built a test plant in 2020 that allows mixed plastics to be recycled without sorting. That process currently has its own limitations, but the work continues.

Perhaps several of these automated processes can be combined into a comprehensive on-site reclamation system in the near future.

But even if possible, such a contraption is likely to be capital intensive to make and manage, negating the low cost of dropping a bubble curtain tube on the riverbed. BUT perhaps this would be an opportunity for a community fractional-ownership investment model, like a co-op where everyone in the community can contribute to the effort, take advantage of the outputs, and profit from dividends. Does this set up another chain of buts? Absolutely. That's your cue to go looking for more buts on your own. Let's move on for now.

Catching plastic entering estuaries is a great start, but a lot of plastic gets stuck and starts breaking down in rivers before reaching the ocean. This hurts river ecosystems. BUT if the cost of a Bubble Barrier or other appropriate catchment system were inexpensive enough, we could continue to install them further and further upstream.

But at the end of the day, even if we manage to develop magical, cost-effective machinery for getting the majority of plastic out of rivers, there's still more that will slip through. And at our current rate of consumption, that's still too much. BUT it would be a lot easier if we could magically reclaim all the plastic, perfectly sorted, immediately upon consumption.

Now we're into option #2. We could reclaim plastic waste immediately at the point of consumption and never let it get into the environment. Problem solved!

But there are many big problems with this. (Rejoice! Remember, we love big buts.) Let's start with the most obvious problem: humans have proven for generations that we suck at consistently sorting trash and properly recycling. BUT today's inexpensive optical components, processors, and AI applications can allow us to make affordable smart trash bins that take the mental work out of sorting. (If 5.2 billion people have a supercomputer in their pocket in the form of a smartphone today, this isn't an outlandish idea.)

But even if every person had a smart bin to make recycling easier, we can be confident that they still won't prioritize recycling as much as needed to achieve our goal. BUT humans are really, really good at prioritizing things that make them money. Why not combine the smart bin with a compensation system that gives consumers credits of real value based on improved recycling profit margins from getting high-purity inputs?

Sound crazy? Well, let me tell you a story about soda and beer cans in the early 1970s. As drink can manufacturing moved from steel to aluminum, my home state of Michigan implemented a plan that paid money for every reclaimed can. In those days, the sides of streets were carpeted in them. Yeah, it was crazy. Apparently Americans had no compunction about tossing trash out of car windows. I would troll my street every weekend for cans.

It became an adolescent's gold mine. Other kids entered the business, and there was cutthroat competition for every last can we could find. Turf wars were fought over those cans. I'm pretty sure I remember earning a black eye in one battle. Soon, there wasn't a can to be found anywhere.

Some states today have bottle and can deposit laws, which makes reclamation attractive. Industry argues that this increases costs, which are passed on to consumers. And in many places recycling bin programs have replaced the practice. Still, recycling rates in places where consumers get cash for recycled items are significantly higher.

But putting a bounty on every piece of plastic the way Michigan did with cans doesn't seem likely. BUT there are actual companies combining the idea of the smart bin and a rewards system right now.

Cambridge Consultants offers a smart bin that uses image recognition to determine what material an item is made from and helps sort it. There's an associated smartphone app that doles out reward points to the user once the item has been correctly deposited. Points can be spent in various ways, including donations to charity.

The Garbi smart recycling bin takes this a step further. It identifies items, sorts them, and can then add them to a shopping list. It can even order delivery through Instacart, Amazon, and Amazon Fresh.

Another product, aptly named The Smart Bin, measures the weight of the material collected, calculates the amount of carbon saved by recycling, and grants rewards points.

But even if everyone on Earth had a smart bin and every river in every country were effectively filtered for trash, millions of tons of plastic would still slip into the oceans every year. And there's already too much plastic out there to begin with.

This takes us to option #3: magically make the plastic disappear after it reaches the sea, or transform it into a substance that won't hurt the ecosystem.

Microorganisms have evolved to break down almost everything in the natural world. They even help metals oxidize. The problem with plastics isn't that they can't be degraded into basic molecules. It's that they've been so recently introduced to the environment that no microorganisms have evolved to use them as a food source. Or so we thought.

In 2016, researchers in Japan discovered a bacteria called *Ideonella sakaiensis*, which they found living on discarded bottles and using the plastic as an energy source. Studying these bacteria led researchers at UT Austin to design the so-called Super Enzymes mentioned earlier. In other research, the University of Sydney discovered that two fungi can turn some plastic into carbon dioxide and harmless monomers. There are now 28 known species of fungi that can degrade plastics. And now waxworms have been found to eat polyethylene plastic bags, while some kinds of mealworms have been found to eat Styrofoam.

So maybe the microbiome will evolve to clean up our mess for us. Or as the AI-driven genetics work suggests, perhaps we can turbocharge Mother Nature and design superorganisms that will make a meal of all kinds of plastic.

But wait! What about the unintended consequences of releasing these organisms into the environment? And in any event, we don't want to wait for Mother Nature to solve our problems. BUT we can do some other things to clean up the mess that's already in the ocean.

In 2012, a Dutch teenager named Boyan Slat gave a TEDx Talk and proclaimed that we could clean the Great Pacific Garbage Patch—the one that Captain Moore discovered and later said was part of the plastic problem we couldn't solve—in five years' time. He was wrong about the timeframe. BUT, the organization he started, the Ocean Cleanup company, has removed 200 metric tons of plastic from the North Pacific so far, using a giant flexible ocean skimmer stretched between two ships.

But that's about only two-tenths of a percent of all the plastic out there, and the garbage patch is still growing. BUT the team is working on a system that's supposed to be three times bigger.

But critics are concerned that the system catches living organisms along with the plastic. And while the company says that the system creates a downward current flow that allows fish to swim below the skimmer, they do find plenty of fish, crabs, and other organisms caught in it. BUT the company says that it's working on ways to reduce this.

But the basic design of the skimmer makes it unlikely that disrupting marine life can be avoided completely. Sea urchins, sea stars, and other creatures are now mixed up in the plastic. Some even attach their eggs to it. What's the 2But here?

While they aren't giving up on their work in the Garbage Patch, Ocean Cleanup has turned its attention to river cleanup. They run skimming operations on rivers like the Ozama in the Dominican Republic, which is one of the most polluted rivers in the world. Ocean Cleanup has managed to collect 10 times more plastic from rivers than from its ocean operation. So, as we've discussed, sometimes we find one chain of buts crossing into a parallel chain. In this case, ocean cleanup leads back to river cleanup.

But even though as much as 80 percent of ocean plastic comes from rivers and coastlines, 20 percent comes from maritime waste. Fishing. And this stuff is the worst.

Discarded plastic fishing nets called ghost nets entangle marine life of all kinds and can damage coral reefs. They are an abomination. Other trash, like plastic filament from broken fishing line, bottles, and other plastic gear thrown overboard from ocean vessels, make up the rest.

Here we could say that the obvious 2But is, "BUT we could encourage fishermen to not use plastic ghost nets, find solutions to the problem of broken fishing lines, and in general be responsible for their trash." BUT in this case, a much more fun solution comes from the 1990s movie *Austin Powers*. We could arm the fish with "*frickin'* laser beams attached to their heads." This would allow them to cut through ghost nets and…maybe bring the ecosystem back into balance by reducing the population of plastic-polluting fishermen. Just kidding. Fishermen are full of plastic and not a healthy meal for well-armed fish.

But the presence of a patently silly but, and a good bit of science fiction, suggests that cleaning up the 100 million metric tons of plastic that's already in the ocean is going to be a real pain in the *but*. BUT there's one more option for at least not making it worse.

Option #4: Humans consume 300 million metric tons of plastic annually. Massively reducing the flow of ocean plastic (and reducing terrestrial pollution while we're at it) would be effectively accomplished if we simply...stopped doing that. Easy peasy. Simple solution, right?

There's a common refrain among plastic pollution experts: the best way to keep plastic out of rivers, oceans, and the environment is to make less of it. But we aren't doing that. Captain Moore himself admits that humans have demonstrated no ability to stop using plastic, and an industry that employs a million people and generates $100 billion in revenue in the United States alone relies on us continuing to use it.

With plastic so pervasive, it's unrealistic to expect that some of it won't wind up in the environment. More like a lot of it. (We are messy creatures.)

Even anti-plastic advocates, the ones who carry around silverware and won't hold a plastic cup when asked, admit that it's "almost impossible" to be a perfectly plastic-free person today.

BUT we should remember that the world lived without plastics until well into the 20th century, which is really not that long ago. And there are tons of new products and packaging options that use alternatives to plastic.

The green straws you find in Starbucks today are made from polylactic acid (PLA), a biodegradable bioplastic made from cornstarch or sugarcane. PLA is somewhat more expensive than some alternatives, and it melts at a lower temperature, but it doesn't go mushy and fall apart like Starbucks' short-lived attempt at cellulose-based straws. PLA is also used in some 3D printing applications.

Corn bioplastic is a relatively new material that can be used for food packaging, even utensils. It's inexpensive and biodegrades in about two to three months.

There's an invasive brown seaweed called wakame in Australia that can be an alternative to plastic wrap. It's edible and decomposes after two weeks.

There are alternatives for hard plastics, soft plastics, shiny plastics, high-temperature plastics, and clear plastics. You've probably noticed that the polystyrene "shipping popcorn" (aka package peanuts) you used to find in boxes has been replaced with either a starch-based popcorn (delicious), air pillows, clever cardboard formations, or even mycelium-based "mushroom popcorn." If there's a plastic product out there, someone is likely working on finding an alternative that can be commercially viable at scale.

There are also a growing number of ways to make plastics that break down faster. A commercial plastic additive called Evanesto will allow single-use plastic products like yogurt cups to break down in a normal backyard compost bin in roughly 300 days.

But, there are clearly a ton of other *buts* to consider with each of these alternatives. And there are plenty of chemists and other scientists voicing skepticism and concern over the prospect of enzymatic solutions, biodegradation accelerant additives, and alternative materials.

BUT Momentum Thinking suggests that there is reason for hope in this. Scientists and engineers, working in cultures that understand and accept the Two But Rule (and don't maintain a no-buts policy), are like those plastic-munching enzymes. They can use their powerful buts to break down problems and continuously find new solutions. Just as AI is improving those Super Enzymes, making them faster, we know that the Two But Rule is the way to accelerate the process of turning buts into breakthroughs.

But none of these projects—from the Great Bubble Barrier to smart bins to fish with frikkin' laser beams on their heads—are yet putting even a tiny dent in the global plastic problem. BUT, as John Hagel points out in *The Journey Beyond Fear*, there is enormous power in telling stories like these. Showing real deployments, even small ones, reduces uncertainty, reinjects momentum, and encourages others to support the work. And telling the whole story openly, including all the 1 Buts and 2 Buts, can make it more powerful and actionable. A great way to turn doubt and skepticism into support and action is to preemptively show your whole hand: what works, what doesn't work, what doesn't work yet, what can scale, what can't, and what we don't yet know how to solve.

For every one of these stories—both the practical ones and the seemingly crazy ones—there are many more buts to explore. More than could fit on the pages of this book before it wound up becoming its own mountain of paper waste. The rest are for you to discover.

An academic paper published in the journal *Science* in 2020 projected the impacts of various methods for reducing environmental plastic by 2040. Here's the quote that stood out to me: "Our analysis indicates that urgent and coordinated action combining pre- and post-consumption solutions could reverse the increasing trend of environmental plastic pollution." I don't know about you, but these kinds of statements drive me crazy. They might be talking about the overabundance of plastic, but they demonstrate a serious scarcity in their supply of buts. That's odd, because there are so many of them! But the petroleum industry really likes to make money. How are you going to get them to play ball and willingly take steps that would make them less money? But most plastic alternatives are still more expensive for manufacturers and less effective, convenient, or appealing to consumers. You can shame or cajole some people into spending more for less, but especially in the parts of the world suffering under tight economic conditions, there are plenty of people who will kill a turtle to save a dime. Especially when they don't have to watch the turtle choke out on their plastic...assuming they never search YouTube for "turtle suffocating on plastic." (Seriously, don't search for that unless you're prepared to see some horrible stuff.)

This is a book that I hope has delivered a few good reasons why we need to reintroduce more buts to our lives—and provided a few ways to do it. So when an expert in industry, academia, or government tells you that the solution to a gnarly problem is "joining together in a comprehensive approach…blah blah blah," you can tell them to show you their buts so that you can "join together" in uncovering more. (And be sure to tell them to ensure that the total number of buts is always divisible by, yeah, two.)

When I started researching this topic, I was daunted by the magnitude of the problem. Then I noticed something. People doing real things to solve the plastic problem are *everywhere*. Their numbers are growing rapidly. And a lot of them have an engineer's love of processing an endless chain of buts into an endless series of solutions.

The ultimate BUT is this: we can work on all these approaches and keep trying more, learning more, until the job's done. And while society seems to take forever to change habits and priorities, some critical generational shifts have already happened in large parts of the world. We might have just enough time left on the ecological "time's up" clock for the rising Clean Generation— the greatest generation of cleanup artists ever to walk the Earth—to finally prioritize the work and fix the mess we all made.

CHAPTER

17

The Rear End

If you've managed to get this far reading a book about buts, then you are my kind of weirdo. Welcome to the Royal Society of But-Heads.

It's time I let you in on our secret mission and give you your assignment. We are here to save the world...with our super-charged buts. That might sound ridiculous, but it really isn't. We have big problems ahead, and we have an even bigger problem with knuckleheads making those problems worse with *half-assed* solutions. The world needs whole-assed solutions, and we can supply that with our masterful application of the Two But Rule.

Your assignment, if you choose to accept it, is to pick a big problem facing humanity and find all the ideas for solving it you can. Make up a few of your own. Then get to work joyously uncovering all the 1Buts, adding 2Buts, which reveal 3Buts, which point to 4Buts, and so on. Then find the even-numbered buts you can do something about, get off your *but*, and go kick some ass.

The Buts We Leave Behind

Having read this book, you might be wondering if you can expect to begin a long and uninterrupted string of effortless successes. Of course not. But at least you know that failure occurs only on an odd-numbered but. Unless you've succeeded at everything in life, you have, at one time or another, left an odd-numbered but behind and moved on. There's nothing wrong with that. All the buts in the world won't prevent you from making mistakes or getting to a place where you just have to call it quits. Yet, even long after the bitter end of a failed effort, remember that the universe keeps a special 2But always ready for a rainy day: BUT life goes on.

As we've seen throughout this book, it's not only common but necessary and worthwhile to explore—and re-explore— things that seem crazy, improbable, or outright impossible. You never know when a new 2But will appear to solve an old, almost forgotten 1But. Never stop looking.

Embrace Yourself

Failure might come on an odd-numbered but, but by now I hope we can agree that true success rarely arrives without encountering any buts at all. Momentum Thinking won't make your new idea any less dumb than the ones you had before. But I hope now you have a repeatable and easy-to-remember way to turn some of them into brilliant successes.

John Kander and Fred Ebb were one of Broadway's greatest collaborative teams, with credits including the musicals *Cabaret* and *Chicago*. They wrote one of their most famous anthems, "New York, New York," for the 1977 film of the same name. Or rather, they wrote a song for the movie that star Robert DeNiro didn't like.

So they went back and reworked it into a masterpiece. Years after Ebb's death, Kander collaborated with Lin Manuel Miranda on a new Broadway production of *New York, New York*. Of his ability to work with both Miranda and Ebb, Kander said this: "The ideas can be terrible, and nobody is a bad person because they had it…BUT you write it and then you change it."

For Kander, like most great artists, it's about the craft, the carpentry. You start with something, make it better as you work, and in the process make yourself better. That is the essence of Momentum Thinking.

All Your Wonderful Buts

Well, that's it. You've arrived at the rear end of *The Two But Rule*. I hope that you were able to learn and pass on a few good *but* jokes—they kill at any pre-teen birthday party—and that you didn't get stuck in too many buts along the way.

The Two But Rule is about a serious subject. Society's failure to soberly embrace negative thinking in the pursuit of positive solutions leads constantly to tragic results. That's why I took a cue from Shakespeare and opted to tell the story with a bit of comedy.

Whether you found yourself chuckling, smirking, scowling, or shooting milk out of your nose at all of those stupid but jokes, I hope your world is now a little safer to express, embrace, and explore all of your wonderful buts.

Acknowledgments

Writing *The Two But Rule* has been a journey of discovery, reflection, and growth. It would not have been possible without the support, guidance, and encouragement of many individuals.

I'd like to extend my deepest gratitude to Jim Minatel at Wiley for taking a chance on a "big idea" book from a first-time author and for pulling together an amazing team of editors, designers, marketing people, publicists, and distribution managers. Chief among this team of experts, Tracy Brown Hamilton was a joy to work with through months of crafting and editing. She taught me to "think beyond how I think" and get the work out. And I can't forget the design and marketing team, whose book cover "cracks" me up every time. Wiley's degree of support for this project has been mind-blowing, and its commitment to excellence has elevated the quality of the content.

The project would have never gotten off the ground without the dedicated readers of 2buts.com. And special thanks to Ashley Watters, the OG editor of The Two But Rule Substack.

Thanks to longtime friends and colleagues for their advice and input both on this book and over the years: Ryan Anderson, Alex Butler, Dirk Brown, Mike Curry, Jerry Cuomo, Don Dodge, Nick Donofrio, Andreas Freund, Ramesh Gopinath, David Gee, Steve Gold, Juan Llanos, Kris Lichter, Randal Leeb-du Toit,

Brigid McDermott, Mike Nelson, Dirk Nicol, Barney Pell, John Patrick, Kal Patel, Rachel Reinitz, Rick Rommel, Jeff Stein, Jim Spohrer, Kevin Surace, John Seely Brown, James Wiggington, Dan Vermeer Pat Sueltz, Jane Harper, and Ron Woan…, and my dear friend, ChatGPT.

There are several cases in the book that benefited from the help of people with special knowledge of the subject. I'd like to thank the teams at The Great Bubble Barrier, Calendly, IBM, Inrupt, The Third Place, and Aimcast. And a special thank-you to Dr. Duane March for his historic insights.

Finally, thanks to my wonderful family for clear-eyed faith, perseverance, and a continuous supply of laughter. Only an old man aided by young children could produce the treasure-trove of *but* jokes contained here.

About the Author

John Wolpert has served as a CEO, product executive, advisor and writer at the forefront of technology and business innovation. His career spans decades, from the early days of the Web to the rise of artificial intelligence.

John has traveled the world identifying and nurturing groundbreaking ideas long before they hit the mainstream. He founded ride-hailing pioneer Flywheel before most people had smartphones. He charged into open source, Java, AI, and blockchain as a three-time IBMer. And after his first article in *Harvard Business Review* appeared in 2002, he was invited by the Australian government to lead an R&D consortium in life sciences and nanotech that explored the challenges of open innovation. All of these ventures were marked by John's approach to problem-solving that embraces critical thinking to find creative solutions.

Whether it's exploring emerging technology, starting a company, or fixing a broken ceiling fan, for John it's all about understanding the nuances of why ideas don't work and using those insights to turn roadblocks into stepping stones. In a world that often shies away from negativity, John stands up to remind us that it's not about avoiding an idea's problems. It's about leaning into them.

John spends his time on the third planet from Sol with his wife and two human children. You can usually find him living 18 months in the future.

Index

A

Aaron, John (flight controller), 7
action, of buts, 97–104, 126–127
ActivityPub, 150–151
Adobe, 21
adversarial method of debate, 67
Aimcast, 143
Airbnb, 90–91
All-In Podcast, 155–156
AlphaFold, 55–56
Alter, Adam (author), 36–37
Apollo 13, 5, 6–7, 8, 92
artificial intelligence (AI). *See also* ChatGPT
   in business scheduling, 141
   function of, 110–111
   overview of, 108–109
   for plastics, 183
   for protein characterization, 55–56
   regulating, 155–161
   2Buts and, 112
   for virtual interactions, 142–143
Athens, crisis of, 164–168
automobiles, 39, 64–66
Awotona, Tope (entrepreneur), 133–138

B

bacteria, 186
bad buts, 59–68
bad/dumb idea, 19–20, 24–26
balanced polymorphism, 47
Barlow, John Perry (author), 94
because, stating, 11
Benson, David (small business owner), 129–133
Berners-Lee, Tim (inventor), 149
Best Buy, 39–41
Bieberdorf, Kate (reporter), 178
birds, wind energy and, 176–177
Bitcoin, 49, 51
Blank, Steve (entrepreneur), 98
blockchain, 33–34, 48–52
blocking, 83–84
Blue Gene supercomputer, 55
boldness, in buts, 22–24
bravery, in buts, 24–26
browsers, Web, 160
budget, government, 168–173
Budget Wars, 171–173
business
   AI use in, 141, 142–143
   challenges of, 129–133
   locations of, 138–144
   raising capital in, 137

business (*continued*)
    scheduling challenges of, 140
    small, 129–133
    starting, 133–138

C
Cabulous, 40–41, 98–100
Calacanis, Jason (commentator),
    155, 156
Calendly, 133–138
Cambridge Consultants, 186
capital, raising, 137
career changing, 120–127
cellular biology, 72–73
chain of buts, 48–53, 118–127
Chalmers University, 183–184
ChatGPT, 108–111, 157, 169, 170
cheating buts, 63–64
circular arguments, 169–173
Clark, William (explorer), 60–63
Clean Generation, 192
Cleese, John, 79, 80
Coca-Cola, 19–20
cold-start problem, 135–136
collaboration, inter-field, 72–73
compromise, 67, 68
con artists, 63–64
conflict, buts in, 163–173
Congress, 169–173
corn bioplastic, 189
courtship, 75
COVID-19 pandemic, 81,
    129–131, 138–139
CRISPR, 46
Cruzatte, Private, 61
cryptocurrency, 33–34
Cylon, 165

D
Dall-E, 109
debate, adversarial method of, 67
debt ceiling, 169–173
*Debt Limit Through the
    Years*, 169–170

decentralization, 147–151
"A Declaration of the Independence
    of Cyberspace" (Barlow), 94
decoherence, 27
defensiveness, 80
DeNiro, Robert (actor), 194
Dimon, Jamie (CEO), 139
disruptive innovation, 36, 54. *See also*
    innovation

E
Ebb, Fred (writer), 194–195
Edmonson, Amy C. (professor), 22, 23
Ehrhorn, Philip (CTO), 181
emissions standards, 64–66
empathetic but, 86–87
Eupatrids, 164, 165, 166–167
Evanesto, 190
Eveleens, Anne Marieke
    (entrepreneur), 182
everyday but, 116, 117–127
experimentation, of buts, 98
exposing, of buts, 75–77

F
Facebook, 6, 18–19
failure
    of AI, 159
    anger and hatred from, 86
    benefits of, 96
    embracing, 194
    experience in, 32–33
    learning from, 96
    of new direction/movements, 95
    repetition of, 93
    timing and, 95–96
    trial and error and, 131
    Two But Rule following, 7
Fanchraych, Tàl (entrepreneur), 40–41
feature creep, of products, 151–155
filtering, for AI, 160–161
fishing, 188
"Five Whys," of Lean Startup
    approach, 101–103

fixing the fan story, 117–118
Flywheel, 41, 42
Ford, Henry (automotive pioneer), 38–39
Frankl, Victor (psychiatrist), 96
freemium release, 135
Freewrite, 152–153, 154
Friedberg, David (commentator), 155, 156
fungi, 186–187
fuzzy but, 13–15, 183

G
gap, in buts, 73–74
Garbi smart recycling bin, 186
Garcia, Daniel (entrepreneur), 40
Gebbia, Joe (entrepreneur), 90
generations, divisions among, 89–96
genetics, 46
Geschke, Charles (entrepreneur), 21
Ghandi, Mahatma (lawyer), 168
ghost nets, 188
gnarly but, 45–47
Goldblum, Jeff (actor), 85
government, budget buts in, 168–173
Graham, Paul (mentor), 90–91, 126–127
Great Bubble Barrier, 181–182, 184
Great Pacific Garbage Patch, 178, 187
Gregory, Joe (banker), 19
groupthink, 67, 95

H
Hagel, John (author), 190
hairball analogy, 92–93
hammer-thinking, 124–126
Happy (documentary), 122
harms, discovery of, 57
HBB mutations, 46–47
Hoplites, 165–166, 167
horse racing analogy, 123
how/what/why problem, 73–74

humor, 80, 81
hypothesis, 26

I
IBM, 55
IDEO, 82–84
Ideonella sakaiensis, 186–187
Independence Day (film), 85
innovation, 28, 35, 36, 54, 68
intention
   in 2But, 59–60
   bad, 87–88
   Best Buy and, 39–41
   for blockchain, 49, 50–51
   butting in on, 38–39
   conflicting, 61–62
   empathy and, 86–87
   example of, 35–36
   exposing, 75–77
   gaps regarding, 73–74
   hidden, 56–57
   honoring, 63
   letting go of, 38
   level of, 38
   momentum and, 62, 88
   openness to, 88
   pain regarding, 36–38
   for plastic reduction, 179
   presenting, 39–41
   of remote-forever employers/employees, 138–139
   of return-to-the-office employers/employees, 138–141
   risk regarding, 36
   Uber and, 41–44
   understanding regarding, 123
inter-field collaboration, 72–73
internal press release, 146
isolation, 81, 143–144

J
jailbreaking, 100
James, Anthony (scientist), 46–47
Jefferson, Thomas (President), 60

Jeong, Ken (actor), 122–123, 126
Jobs, Steve (CEO), 21
Johnston, JJ (business partner), 131
juxtaposition, 80

K
Kander, John (writer), 194–195
Kelley, David (entrepreneur), 82
killer phrases, 27, 28
King, Martin Luther, Jr.
        (activist), 168
Ko, Anthony (entrepreneur), 40
Kogan, Aleksandr (researcher), 18
Kranz, Gene (flight director), 5
Krishna, Arvind (CEO), 23
Kuhn, Thomas (author), 53

L
large language model (LLM), 108
lean NOx trap (LNT), 64–66
Lean Startup approach, 98–103
Lehman Brothers, 19
Lessin, Sam (entrepreneur), 137
Lewis, Meriwether (explorer), 60–63
logical gap, 74
logistics network, dilemmas
        regarding, 76
Lyft, 154–155

M
MacKenzie, Gordon (author), 92
malaria, 46
management, of buts, 105–111, 112
Manson, Mark (author), 96
March, Duane (academic), 164
Marieke Eveleens, Anne
        (entrepreneur), 182
Mastodon, 149–150
McAllister, Ian (businessman), 146
mealworm, 187
meetings, scheduling for, 143
Mercedes Benz, 66
Meta, 150
microorganisms, 186

microplastics, 178. *See also* plastics
mindfulness, 37–38, 52–53
minimally viable product (MVP),
        98–99, 101
Miranda, Lin Manuel (actor), 195
Missouri River, 60–61
Model T (Ford), 39
momentum, 62, 74, 88
Momentum Thinking, xiv, 4, 8,
        52–53, 97. *See also*
        Two But Rule
Moore, Charles (chemist), 178
mosquitoes, 46–47
motivation, 87–88
Musk, Elon (CEO), 13–15, 183

N
Nadella, Satya (CEO), 23
nanotech, 72–73
new direction/movements, 92–93, 95
New York, New York, 195
no-buts policy, 17–18, 19–21,
        27, 28
non-negotiables, 120, 122
Nostr, 149–150
null hypothesis, 26

O
ocean, 178–182, 186–188
Ocean Cleanup, 187
odious but, 85–86
old but problem, 89–96
1But
    answers for, 93
    avoiding, 10
    challenges of, 29
    conflict in, 67
    leaving behind, 194
    rescue of, 30
    rewards for, 101
    stating, 9–11
    summarizing, 86–87
    value of, 30
    variations of, 8, 9–10

open sandbox testing service, for
    AI, 158–159
OpenAI, 108–109
orbit analogy, 92–93
organizational gap, 74

P
Palihapitiya, Chamath
    (commentator), 155, 156
Parakilas, Sandy (whistleblower), 18
parenting purgatory story, 118–120
patient zero, 43–44
peer-to-peer file sharing, 66
Peisistratus, 168
Perls, Dana (businesswoman),
    46–47
plastics
    AI and, 183
    alternatives for, 189–190
    breaking down of, 186–187
    consumption of, 188–189
    disposing of, 182
    Evanesto for, 190
    filters for, 180
    fuzzy but regarding, 183
    ghost nets, 188
    Great Bubble Barrier
        for, 181–182
    intention regarding, 179
    marine life and, 178
    micro-, 178
    production of, 189
    proteins and, 183
    reclaiming, 184–185
    recycling of, 183–186
    reduction methods for, 191
    in rivers, 179–180
    sorting of, 182, 183
    statistics regarding, 178, 188–189
    Super Enzyme and, 183
polylactic acid (PLA), 189
poopy diaper analogy, 116
Portugal, Treaty of Tordesillas
    and, 57

positivity sandwich, 87
press release, internal, 146
products
    control of, 146–151
    core philosophy focus of, 153, 154
    decentralization of, 147–151
    feature creep of, 151–155
    overview of, 145
    regulating AI in, 155–161
    review, 2Buts for, 146
    social networks as, 146–151
protection, of buts, 111
proteins, 54–56, 183
psychological safety, 22–23

Q
quantum computing, 27–28

R
Railware, 134–135
R&D contracts, 77
reality TV, 171
reclamation, 185
recycling, 183–186
rediscovery, of buts, 53–54
reMarkable, 152, 153–154, 155
remote work, 138–140
remote-forever proponent, intention
    of, 141–144
return-to-the-office proponent,
    intention of, 138–141
ride-sharing app, 41–44, 55, 76, 136
Ries, Eric (startup guru), 98
rivers, plastic in, 179–180,
    181–182, 188
Rosenberg, Marshall
    (psychologist), 86
runaway buts, 92–95

S
Sacks, David (commentator),
    155, 156
sandboxing, of AI, 158–159
Santayana, George, 91

SARS COV-2, 73
scheduling, 140, 141
science, 53–54
science, of buts, 26
security, of buts, 111
sickle cell anemia, 46, 47
skimmer, ocean, 187–188
Slack, 136
Slat, Boyan, 187
small business, 129–133. *See also* business
smart bin, 184–186
The Smart Bin, 186
so that, finding, 41–42, 44
social life, of buts, 71, 72–73
social networking, 146–151
SOLID Pods, 149
Solon, 163–168
SpaceX, 13–15, 183
Spain, Treaty of Tordesillas and, 57
Spanx, 20
stagnation, 36–37
Star Trek, 63
startups, 89, 98–99, 126, 133–138. *See also specific startups*
straws, 189
Substack, 148–149
Super Enzyme, 183, 186–187
supply chain network, 76

T
taxis, 40–41, 42–43, 98–100, 126
team, 80–84, 101, 143–144
technical gap, 73–74
testing, of buts, 98
Thetes, 165, 166, 167
The Third Place (coffee shop), 129–133
This is Your Digital Life, 18
Threads, 150–151
301 redirect, 148–149
timing, for buts, 82–84, 106–107
toxic positivity inferno, 23

Treaty of Tordesillas, 57
trial and error, 131
Twitter, 146–151
Two But Rule. *See also* Momentum Thinking
  basis of, 4–5
  benefits of, 4, 31–34
  chain of buts in, 48–53
  odd-numbers in, 7, 52, 67
  overview of, 3–5, 7–8
  process of, 102–103
  as subtle art, 59
  training for, 144
2But
  because statement for, 11
  in career changing, 120–127
  ChatGPT for, 109–111
  example of, 8
  first principles regarding, 13–15
  in fixing the fan story, 117–118
  formulating, 84–85
  as fuzzy, 13–15
  intention reveal in, 59–60
  for non-negotiables, 122
  notation of, 107
  in parenting purgatory story, 118–120
  prompts for, 110
  stating, 12–13
  tools for, 106–107
  variations of, 12
tyranny, 165

U
Uber, 41–44, 136, 155
UN Global Plastics Treaty, 182
University of Sydney, 186–187
University of Texas at Austin, 183

V
Volkswagen, 64–66

W

wakame, 189
Warnock, John (entrepreneur), 21
watchdog system, for AI, 157
waxworm, 187
Web3, 94–95
wind energy, 176–177
Winterkorn, Martin (CEO), 65
working backwards approach,
    146

World Wide Web, 94,
    159–160

Y

Y Combinator, 89, 90
yeah-butting, 84–85

Z

Zero Knowledge cryptography, 161
Zuckerberg, Mark (CEO), 18–19, 150